DELICIOUSLY HOLISTIC COOKBOOK

HEALING FOODS RECIPES AND LIFESTYLE TIPS TO HELP INCREASE YOUR ENERGY AND IMMUNITY!

SHELLEY ALEXANDER, CHFS

Deliciously Holistic **by Shelley Alexander**

Copyright © 2013 by Shelley Alexander

Text, Photography, and Food Styling by Shelley Alexander © 2013

First published in the United States in 2013 by In Harmony Publishing.
All rights reserved.

No part of this book may be used or reproduced in any manner whatsoever
without prior permission in writing from the publisher except in the case
of brief quotations embodied in critical articles and reviews.

For information please contact aharmonyhealing@gmail.com
www.aharmonyhealing.com

ISBN 978-0-9846908-0-0
ISBN: 0984690808

1. Healing Foods 2. Cooking 3. Health 4. Diet 5. Nutrition 6. Weight Loss

Library of Congress Cataloging–in–Publication Data 2010906326
Los Angeles, California

Alexander, Shelley

Deliciously Holistic: Healing Foods Recipes And Lifestyle Tips To Help Increase
Your Energy And Immunity/Shelley Alexander.

DEDICATION

I would like to thank my mom for being my biggest supporter and cheerleader. Thank you for instilling in me a passion for delicious real foods and for teaching me how to cook. I love you!

DELICIOUSLY HOLISTIC

TABLE OF CONTENTS

THE PURPOSE OF THIS HOLISTIC COOKBOOK	14
MY PERSONAL STORY	16
TOP REASONS TO BUY SEASONAL, LOCAL, ORGANIC FOODS	18
WHOLE FOODS DEFINITIONS	20
HOLISTIC SHOPPING GUIDE	22
TIPS FOR MAKING HEALTHY FOOD PREPARATION QUICK AND CONVENIENT	24
PANTRY STAPLES FOR THE HOLISTIC KITCHEN	26
RECOMMENDED ONLINE RESOURCES	28
RECOMMENDED HEALTHY FATS AND OILS	30
RECOMMENDED NATURAL SWEETENERS	32
FLAVOR ENHANCERS WITH HEALTH ADVANTAGES	34
HEALTHY PREPARED FOODS OPTIONS	38
UNIQUE SUPERFOODS FOR ENERGY, STRENGTH, AND IMMUNITY	40
HEALTHY BEVERAGES TO GET THE GLOW	42
SMOKE POINT OF OILS FOR COOKING	43
KITCHEN EQUIPMENT	44
IMPORTANT NOTE ABOUT FRESH FRUITS AND VEGETABLES	46
IMPORTANT TIPS FOR IMPROVING YOUR DIGESTIVE HEALTH	47

HOLISTIC RECIPES

8 SEASONAL MENUS

Fall   Winter   Spring   Summer   48

ESSENTIAL BASICS

(V) stands for vegan recipes (RV) stands for raw vegan recipes

Spiced Maple Syrup (V)   57

Clarified Butter   57

Cultured Probiotic Vegetables (RV)   58

Oven-Dried Tomatoes (V)   60

Blood Orange Coconut Butter (RV)   61

Meyer Lemon Coconut Butter (RV)   61

Roasted Garlic Coconut Butter (V)   61

3-Herb Pesto (RV)   62

Arugula Spinach Walnut Pesto (RV)   62

Fresh and Cultured Mayonnaise   63

White Balsamic Mayonnaise   63

Honey Dijon Mayonnaise   63

Thai Basil Lime Mayonnaise   63

Yogurt Goat Cheese and Whey   64

Tomato Tarragon Goat Cheese   64

Lemon Dill Goat Cheese   64

Cultured Tomato Pineapple Salsa (RV)   65

Cultured Apple Goji Berry Compote (RV)   66

DREAMY DRINKS

■ CREAMY NUT AND SEED MILKS — 70

Recipe and Guidelines for Soaking Nuts and Seeds — 71

Carrot Pecan Milk (RV) — 72

Orange Ginger Pumpkin Seed Milk (RV) — 74

Vanilla Brazil Nut Milk (RV) — 74

Mango Cashew Milk (RV) — 75

Nectarine Walnut Milk (RV) — 75

Banana Hemp Milk (RV) — 77

Carob Almond Milk (RV) — 78

Vanilla Pistachio Milk (RV) — 78

Coconut Milk 2 Ways (RV) — 79

■ GREEN ENERGY SMOOTHIES — 80

Bing Cherry Smoothie (RV) — 81

Wild Blueberry Smoothie (RV) — 82

Peach Cucumber Smoothie (RV) — 84

Strawberry Banana Maca Smoothie (RV) — 84

Papaya Smoothie (RV) — 85

Chocolate Raspberry Smoothie (RV) — 87

Mango Raspberry Spirulina Smoothie (RV) — 88

Acai Berry Cranberry Smoothie (RV) — 89

Cherry Goji Berry Smoothie (RV) — 90

Blueberry Pomegranate Smoothie (RV) — 91

Nectarine Smoothie (RV) — 91

■ Amazing Elixirs, Tonics, and Cultured Drinks 92

Peach Lemonade Elixir (RV) 93

E3 Live Melon Elixir (RV) 94

Vanilla Cardamom Coconut Kefir (RV) 95

Cinnamon Almond Coconut Kefir (RV) 95

Pineapple Coconut Kefir (RV) 96

Chia Milk Kefir 96

Carrot Orange Tonic (RV) 97

Hazelnut Herbal Coffee (V) 97

Grapefruit Kombucha Tea Soda (RV) 98

Spiced Milk Tea Tonic (V) 99

Lemon Ginger Tulsi Tea (V) 99

BOUNTIFUL BREAKFASTS

■ Quick Breakfasts 100

Mango Chia Ginger Granola (RV) 101

Orange Coconut Yogurt (RV) 103

Berries and Cream (RV) 105

Raw Seed or Nut Cream (RV) 105

Pear Pomegranate Nut Bowl (RV) 107

Nectarine Yogurt Parfait 109

Cranberry Quinoa Cereal (V)   111

French Toast with Spiced Blueberry Syrup   113

Buckwheat Fruit Granola (V)   115

Buttermilk Millet Waffles   117

Chai Pumpkin Oatmeal (V)   118

Basic Grits (V)   120

Balsamic Brown Butter Grits   120

Green Leaf Lettuce, Tomato, and Onion Scramble   121

Rainbow Chard Omelet   123

Caramelized Balsamic Onion Scramble   124

Yellow Squash and Basil Omelet   125

SATISYFING SOUPS AND STOCKS

Chicken Stock   127

Roasted Chicken Stock   127

Beef Stock   128

Vegetable Stock (V)   129

Corn Stock (V)   130

Tomato Basil Cream Soup   131

Pumpkin Hazelnut Chai Soup (V)   133

Sweet Potato Maple Soup (V)   135

Raw Corn Chowder (RV)   137

Raw Watermelon Jicama Soup (RV)   139

Chicken Coconut Soup   140

SUMPTUOUS SALADS WITH IRRESISTIBLE VINAIGRETTES AND DRESSINGS

Meyer Lemon Miso Dressing (RV)	142
Blood Orange Maple Dressing (V)	142
Aged Balsamic Vinaigrette (RV)	143
Clementine Cassis Dressing (RV)	144
Clementine Champagne Dressing (RV)	144
Cherry Almond Dressing (RV)	145
Meyer Lemon Champagne Vinaigrette (RV)	145
Mango Ginger Dressing (RV)	146
Heirloom Tomato Cream Dressing (RV)	147
Goji Berry Kombucha Dressing (RV)	147
Carrot Tahini Dressing (RV)	148
Blood Orange, Ambrosia Apple, and Baby Spinach Salad (RV)	149
Cranberry Tuna Salad	150
Chicken Vegetable Quinoa Salad	151
Arugula Comice Pear Salad (RV)	152
Watermelon Radish, Golden Beet, and Watercress Salad (RV)	153
Raw Beet Tartare (RV)	155
Red Cabbage Apple Salad (RV)	157
Butternut Squash Mixed Baby Greens Salad	158
Italian Vegetable Salad with Black Pepper Croutons (V)	159
Hemp Seed Herb Salad (RV)	160
Fuji Apple Salad	163
Yuzu Cucumber Salad (RV)	164

SENSATIONAL SANDWICHES, WRAPS, AND ROLLS

Wild Salmon Vegetable Rolls 166

Sardine Lettuce Wraps 167

Mixed Vegetable Pea Shoots Sandwich (V) 168

Romaine Tacos (RV) 169

Portobello Mushroom and Grilled Onion Burger (V) 170

DELECTABLE DINNER ENTRÉES

Wild Salmon Patties 172

Lemon Herb Wild Black Cod 173

Lemongrass Ginger Wild Salmon 175

3-Herb Pesto Wild Halibut 176

Lime Miso Cornish Game Hens 177

Dijon Honey Chicken Wings 178

Mole Chili 180

Beef Ragu 182

Vegetable Marinara Sauce (V) 182

Lamb Chops with Spicy Mint Chutney 183

Slow Braised Beef Roast 185

Carrot Walnut Cream Fettuccine (RV) 186

Basil Alfredo with Zucchini Noodles (RV) 188

SUCCULENT SIDE DISHES

Brown Rice Pilaf   190

Black Rice Pilaf   190

Potato Parsley Mash   191

Shitake Mushroom Sauté   192

Basil Garlic Spinach   193

Garlic Collard Greens   194

Zucchini Onion Sauté (V)   195

Purple Cauliflower Mash   196

Slow-Cooked Black-Eyed Peas   197

Mustard and Turnip Greens with Roasted Baby Turnips   198

Pomegranate Millet Pilaf   199

Barbecue Sweet Potato Fries (V)   200

Roasted Lemon Fennel and Onions (V)   201

SUPER SNACKS

Sweet Potatoes with Coconut Cinnamon Sprinkle (V)   203

Spicy Guacamole (RV)   205

Smoky Orange Hummus (V)   207

Encrusted Goat Cheese   208

Cultured Vegetable Dip (RV)   209

Carob Pecan Spread (RV)   209

Pumpkin Seed Spread (RV)   210

Chive Deviled Eggs   212

DELICIOUS DESSERTS

Raw Chocolate Mousse (RV)   214

Raspberry Chocolate Mousse Pie (RV)   215

Hot Fudge Sauce (RV)   216

Fudge Goji Berry Truffles (RV)   217

Strawberry Frozen Yogurt with Balsamic Syrup   218

Piña Colada Ice Cream (RV)   219

Piña Colada Ice Cream Float (RV)   219

Mango Ice Cream (RV)   220

Papaya Ice Cream (RV)   220

Banana Coconut Chia Pudding (V)   221

Acai Berry Cranberry Tea Sherbet (V)   223

Carob Almond Chia Pudding (RV)   225

Plum Crumble (RV)   226

Pumpkin Raisin Hemp Bread Pudding   227

METRIC CONVERSION CHART   229

ABOUT THE AUTHOR   230

THE PURPOSE OF THIS HOLISTIC COOKBOOK

My wish is to help you experience the joy that comes with eating delicious whole foods that will help you feel and look your best.

Today, there is so much information on the Internet and in diet and health books about what you should and shouldn't eat. It can be extremely confusing and frustrating for many people who care about having good health and just want to make realistic choices to help them with this goal.

By now, you may be starting to realize that the standard American diet of refined and heavily processed unnatural foods will not allow you to achieve and maintain vibrant health. But is there a simple way of eating that can give you the energy, strength, and immunity you need to experience vibrant health?

Is it vegan? Is it paleo or primal? Is it vegetarian?

As a Holistic Chef and Certified Healing Foods Specialist, I truly believe you need to eat in a holistic, natural way that nourishes, strengthens, energizes, and helps heal your body while working for your individual lifestyle and health goals. What this way of eating should consist of is an abundance of fresh, seasonal, nutrient-rich, sustainable, local, organic whole foods that are a great pleasure for you to eat. These foods should be produced in a way that supports your health and the environment.

Once you begin to eat in this holistic way, constant hunger, overeating, and intense cravings will no longer be an issue, as your body receives all the nourishment and nutrients it needs to feel completely satisfied. You will no longer want to buy or eat highly processed foods that have chemicals, artificial preservatives, artificial flavors, artificial colors, pesticides, antibiotics, growth hormones, genetically modified ingredients, unnatural fillers, high heat extracted, hydrogenated, or chemically processed vegetable oils, artificial and refined sweeteners, refined grains, and factory-farm-raised animals that have been treated poorly and fed unnatural diets. When you eat these unnatural types of foods, you will not provide the nutritional foundation you need to achieve and maintain vibrant health.

My cookbook is written from a chef's perspective and as a true lover of real foods that taste good and appeal to all your senses. But equally critical to me are the power and importance of eating healing whole foods for optimum health.

With my holistic cookbook, you will learn to eat and cook with delicious whole foods that I specifically chose to provide important health benefits to your body. You may choose from a wonderful array of fresh, seasonal, organic fruits, vegetables, herbs, spices, nuts, seeds, whole grains, raw and organic dairy, pasture-raised animals and eggs, and sustainable wild seafood.

This cookbook includes many of the nourishing recipes I personally love and health tips that I give to family, friends, and clients I have worked with via my company, A Harmony Healing, who want to wean themselves off a diet of heavily processed foods filled with unnatural ingredients to a natural holistic way of eating that is full of nutrients for good health.

This cookbook will help you enjoy wonderful foods that taste great, but are not too time consuming to create and are easy to incorporate into your busy life.

You will find that my recipes are designed to be straightforward and easy to prepare. I have included some of my traditional favorite family recipes with my new twists. I've also created many new recipes that use ingredients and flavor combinations influenced by my food experiences in California.

There are over 100 wonderful recipes that are raw and cooked vegan. By using all of these plant-based recipes, you will be able to increase your intake of amazing plant superfoods and learn how to balance these plant foods with ethically produced meat, seafood, egg, and dairy options.

If you are confused and frustrated with fad diets and quick-fix weight-loss plans, then this book will help you find a natural way of eating for life that will allow you to start achieving and maintaining your ideal body weight without counting calories and measuring every bite you put in your mouth. I purposely left out calorie counts, protein, carbohydrate, and fat gram information so that you will learn to start instinctively listening to what your body needs rather than totally focusing in on how many calories, protein, carbohydrates, or fat grams each recipe has. Eating in this way is totally liberating and will help you start truly enjoying the gift of nutrient-rich whole foods and the power they have to heal and rejuvenate your body and mind.

I have eaten and personally used the health-promoting foods, superfoods, and whole foods supplements in this book and have provided the information on their benefits, along with researching the best companies to try, so that I can make your transition to a holistic lifestyle much easier.

Remember that each of us is a unique individual with different tastes, likes, dislikes, needs, and requirements. Relax and enjoy the process of adding delectable new and unfamiliar foods into your daily diet to discover what works for you. Listen to your body and observe how these new daily changes make you feel.

I hope that once you began to eat and live a holistic lifestyle, you will start to truly experience balance, wholeness, and vibrant health in your life! ⌒

My Personal Story

I grew up in Shaker Heights, Ohio, and even though both of my parents worked full time, my parents always made sure that we all sat down to enjoy meals as a family.

On the weekends, my parents loved to host dinner parties for family and friends. Many of the party menus were created from favorite recipes that my mom learned from her mother and grandmother. My mom also created lots of new recipes based on foods that were available in our grandparents' garden and at local area farmers' markets.

To this day, I can still remember eating the crisp green beans, spicy mustard greens, tender turnip greens, earthy collard greens, luscious tomatoes, refreshing cucumbers, sweet and spicy peppers, sweet apples, and juicy grapes grown in my grandparents' garden.

My parents also took us for many Saturday morning visits to the West Side Market to purchase fresh, seasonal, and homemade artisanal foods from the local farmers and food artisans. I still remember being in awe of the massive amounts of glistening, perfectly ripe, colorful fruits and vegetables, tempting cheeses, fragrant exotic spices, vibrant green herbs, fresh-caught seafood, fresh-butchered meats, yummy pastries, and beautiful cakes everywhere that I looked.

I was totally hooked on the wonderful aromas that emanated from every direction. Every vendor was so friendly and generously offered us homemade delectable delicacies to taste and enjoy. I was so excited that I wished I had two stomachs so I could eat everything I saw! All of these trips made me really appreciate the wonderful tastes, colors, and aromas of locally produced foods. After all, these foods were made by the people who had grown them, felt a deep connection to their food, and had great passion for what they produced. Hearing all of their interesting stories really inspired and excited me.

My dad was raised in South Carolina and grew up eating many of the traditional dishes from the South. My dad's Southern favorites were black-eyed peas, fried chicken, braised pork neck bones, beef short ribs, collard greens, spicy cabbage, grits, peach cobbler, sweet potato pie, and cornbread. My dad would always talk about how Southerners have a great appreciation for taking the time to sit down and enjoy delicious, farm-fresh, hearty meals with family and friends. Since Southern foods were my dad's favorite meals, my mom made sure to re-create flavorful versions of all of the dishes he knew and loved.

When I turned eight years old, my mom started teaching me how to cook and assist her in the kitchen. My mom would encourage me to smell, feel, and taste all the foods we made throughout the cooking process. She taught me the importance of cooking instinctively, guided by the flavors and unique properties of each dish we prepared.

Some of my favorite foods I prepared with my mom were waffles, omelets, collard greens, baked chicken with cornbread dressing, local walleye fish, green beans with new potatoes, vanilla bean ice cream, cookies, and apple pie.

Every meal was so exciting and satisfying to me because I couldn't wait to taste the end result of what we accomplished in preparing these delicious foods. Many of the foods I learned to make at home were made with delicious, local produce, local meats, local seafood, and lots of fresh herbs and spices. Preparing these foods with my mom really taught me to appreciate and respect the love and care that goes into creating wonderful meals for your family and friends.

As I grew older, I came to realize that I had developed a great passion for cooking and enjoying food with my family and friends. After I graduated from college with a Bachelor of Science degree in Business Management and Finance, I moved to California and began to work as a pharmaceutical sales representative.

While working as a sales representative, I continued my love affair with food, cooking, and entertaining for my new friends. I was amazed at the vast array of delicious, exotic, fresh fruits, vegetables, seafood, and unique local food products that were available at the farmers' markets year-round in California.

I begin to create many new dishes which took advantage of California's seasonal, locally grown foods. I also loved the fact that California had so many different ethnic foods and globally inspired restaurants to enjoy and explore.

My love of all things food-related led me to go back to school to study the culinary arts. After I graduated from culinary school, I continued my exploration of global cuisine while working at a variety of catering companies and in a restaurant. Once I gained significant work experience in the food industry, I started my own catering and event planning company, Escapade Events, where we prepared globally inspired cuisine for both social and corporate clients.

Eventually, my busy lifestyle, high stress level, eating a diet high in refined convenience foods, infrequent exercise, and sleeping only four to five hours per night began to take a toll on my body. I begin to experience issues with daily indigestion, acid reflux, bloating, weight gain, acne, and low energy levels. On some nights my indigestion and acid reflux were so bad that I had to attempt to sleep sitting up to ease the gas pain and to keep the acid from seeping into my throat. I knew I could not continue to live my life like that because I was miserable.

I also knew from my time spent as a pharmaceutical sales representative that I did not want to start taking prescription medicine just to alleviate the symptoms. I needed to address the underlying issues that were causing my initial health problems, so I began to help my body to heal itself by studying and using holistic healing methods and holistic lifestyle principals.

I started applying stress management techniques, started seriously looking at my lifestyle choices, started walking weekly, got colonics, took whole food supplements, took herbs for the indigestion and acid reflux, and started taking digestive plant enzymes with every meal. I also began eating only whole foods, including raw, probiotic-rich, cultured foods, organic raw and cooked plant foods, wild seafood, organic pasture-raised meats, organic raw dairy, and pastured eggs. I made sure to properly chew and enjoy my meals without rushing or eating under stress.

Gradually my health started to improve as my digestive system began to heal and my body got stronger. I had a few setbacks along the way and experienced some unique reactions that surprised me but I never gave up on my body's amazing ability to rejuvenate and heal. Eventually all of my health issues got better, I lost weight naturally, and I felt strong, vibrant, and filled with energy! I learned so much about how certain foods, drinks, and lifestyle choices can really impact your health positively or negatively depending on what you choose.

My desire to learn more led me to take classes in 2008 to become certified as a *Healing Foods Specialist*. The success of my own healing, combined with my knowledge of holistic foods with healing properties, inspired me to create a holistic food, nutrition, and wellness company, *A Harmony Healing,* so that I could help as many people as possible to learn how to wean themselves off the standard American diet and learn how to easily prepare delicious, real, healing foods and make holistic lifestyle choices that support their health. ✎

Top Reasons to Buy Seasonal, Local, Organic Foods

- Buying seasonal, local, organic foods helps to support our local organic farmers who believe in protecting the planet and raising our food in a sustainable manner.

- Buying seasonal, local, organic foods helps maintains the health and safety of farm workers.

- The nutritional value, quality, taste, and diversity of seasonal, local, organic foods are better than conventional foods.

- Buying seasonal, local, organic foods supports our health, the health of our soil, sustainable agriculture, and ultimately the health of our planet.

- Buying seasonal, local, organic foods helps protect our water supply, oceans, rivers, lakes, and streams from dangerous chemicals, fertilizers, pesticides, herbicides, and antibiotics.

If you can't find a variety of seasonal, local, certified organic foods in your area at local farmers' markets, natural food stores, and co-op markets, seek out your community-supported agriculture groups. You may find that many local farmers have not gone certified organic because of the expense involved but produce food that follows many of the principles of certified organic farmers. Some farmers may also be transitioning to become certified organic and are already practicing the principles of certified organic farmers. If you do have access to seasonal, local, organic foods and still can't see the value of purchasing 100 percent organic, or you can't afford to buy all organic, then you need to at least purchase the foods listed below in organic only. When grown or raised by conventional methods, these foods have high levels of chemical pesticides, herbicides, fertilizers, antibiotics, steroids, animal by-products, genetically modified seeds, and growth hormones that can't be removed. The following produce information comes from the Environmental Working Group's Web site.

TOP REASONS TO BUY SEASONAL, LOCAL, ORGANIC FOODS

- **FRUITS:** apples, blueberries, strawberries, nectarines, grapes, peaches, pears, cucumbers, plums (imported), and cherries.

- **VEGETABLES:** carrots, potatoes, sweet bell peppers, celery, collard greens, spinach, lettuce, green beans, hot peppers, and kale.

- **MEATS, POULTRY, AND DAIRY**

- **BABY FOOD**

The Environmental Working Group has all the information on produce that needs to be avoided in a handy, free, produce guide called the "Dirty Dozen Plus™" and the "Clean 15™." Their Web site is www.ewg.org/foodnews/

To find local, sustainable farmers in your area, look up the Web sites www.localharvest.org and www.eatwellguide.org.

Another cost-effective option for eating organic food is to start your own food garden at your home! You can also start a community garden in your neighborhood with your neighbors. The Web site www.communitygarden.org has good information on how to do this.

WHOLE FOODS DEFINITIONS

I have included these whole foods definitions so that you will know what foods I recommend when you go to purchase them and make the recipes in this cookbook.

COOKED WHOLE FOODS: Nutrient-dense, unprocessed, or minimally processed whole foods prepared for eating through traditional cooking methods which use heat. The foods I recommend for cooking include pasture-raised organic meats and poultry, pastured eggs, organic dairy, sustainable wild seafood, vegetables, fruits, legumes, beans, and organic sprouted or naturally fermented grains.

RAW OR LIVING VEGAN FOODS: Nutrient-dense, unprocessed, or minimally processed whole foods that have not been cooked or heated above 118° F. Living foods are raw foods that have been sprouted, fermented, or cultured. Preparing foods in this way preserves the essential nutrients and enzymes that come in all raw foods. Living foods are easier to digest, and the sprouting, fermenting or culturing process releases important nutrients and makes them available to our body. Our bodies need a balance of both raw and cooked plant foods for good health, energy, and total nutrition. Raw or living foods include raw vegetables, raw fruits, cultured or fermented vegetables and fruits, raw and sprouted nuts and seeds, sprouted legumes, sprouted grains, and raw sea vegetables. The raw vegan recipes are denoted with *Raw Vegan.

COOKED VEGAN FOODS: Nutrient-dense, unprocessed, or minimally processed whole foods prepared for eating through traditional cooking methods which use heat. The cooked vegan foods in this cookbook include vegetables, fruits, whole grains, seeds, beans, and legumes. The cooked vegan recipes are denoted with *Vegan.

LIVE CULTURED OR FERMENTED FOODS AND DRINKS: Originally used by ancient societies as a way to preserve fresh foods and beverages before they had refrigeration, canning, and freezing. Live raw cultured or fermented foods and drinks provide beneficial lactic acid bacteria that act as a natural food preservative. Cultured or fermented foods and drinks are an excellent source of healthy microorganisms or probiotics and enzymes, which help maintain a healthy digestive system. The culturing or fermenting process releases important nutrients and makes it easier for us to digest these foods. Cultured or fermented foods also help strengthen our immune system. Some examples of these foods are coconut kefir, Kombucha tea, raw sauerkraut, beet kvass, and yogurt.

ORGANIC FOODS: According to the U.S. Department of Agriculture, with 100 percent certified organic foods, all the ingredients are certified organic and contain the USDA organic seal. With 95 percent certified organic foods, 5 percent of the ingredients are not organic, and the food contains the USDA organic seal. In foods made with organic ingredients, 75 percent–90 percent of the listed ingredients are organic and do not carry the USDA organic seal. Organic food is produced by farmers who emphasize the conservation of water and soil and the use of renewable resources to enhance environmental quality and conserve biodiversity for future generations.

100 PERCENT CERTIFIED ORGANIC MEATS, POULTRY, DAIRY, AND PRODUCE: According to the USDA, 100 percent certified organic meats, poultry, and dairy carry a USDA organic label, which means no steroids, no growth hormones, no antibiotics, no bioengineering, or irradiation was used. Animals that are organic are fed only an organic diet with no animal by-products. 100 percent certified organic produce carries a USDA organic label, which means the produce is grown without genetically modified seeds, no synthetic fertilizers, no sewage sludge, no conventional pesticides, no herbicides, and no irradiation. Only foods that are certified as at least 95 percent–100 percent organic will have the official USDA organic seal. Certified organic produce label codes begin with a 9.

PASTURE-RAISED OR PASTURED ANIMALS: Pasture-raised animals have been allowed to graze freely outdoors and eat a natural diet of pasture. Pasture-raised animals are the best choice for animal-based protein. Pasture-raised animals are healthier than factory-farm-raised animals because they have not been given any animal by-products, growth hormones, or antibiotics and are raised in a humane manner. The grazing done by pasture-raised animals also helps to improve the quality of the soil by enhancing soil fertility. Pastured dairy comes from grass-fed cows. Pastured eggs come from pasture-raised chickens that have been allowed to roam freely and eat a natural diet of insects and forage. You can locate local suppliers in your area on the Internet.

GRASS-FED ORGANIC MEAT: "Grass-fed" has several definitions. The general term means that an animal has been fed grass at some time during the course of its life. The best choice when purchasing grass-fed meats is to look for 100 percent organic grass-fed, grass-finished meats because this is a good indication that the animal has eaten a totally natural diet of organic grass, hay, and grass seeds for its entire life. "Certified humane" is an additional certification that assures they are raised and handled humanely.

ORGANIC POULTRY AND EGGS: According to the USDA, organic poultry have not been given growth hormones, antibiotics, or animal by-products in their diet. Organic poultry are given organic grains and forage for their diet. Organic eggs come from chickens that have been raised organically. If you can't find pasture-raised chickens in your area, this is your next best option.

HOLISTIC SHOPPING GUIDE

I CREATED THIS GUIDE TO SERVE AS A SHOPPING RESOURCE TO HELP YOU START ON YOUR PATH TO VIBRANT HEALTH AND WELLNESS. IF YOU KNOW THE BEST PLACES TO SHOP FOR WHOLE FOODS, YOU WILL BE ABLE TO START ENJOYING THE BENEFITS OF EATING THESE REAL FOODS AND USING HOLISTIC LIFESTYLE PRODUCTS IN YOUR HOME WHICH SUPPORT YOUR HEALTH AND THE HEALTH OF OUR PLANET.

1. FARMERS' MARKETS: There are many wonderful farmers' markets to explore in cities around the world. I encourage you to try to go to your local area farmers' markets weekly to purchase fresh, local, seasonal, and organic produce and other unique local food products produced by farmers and local food artisans in your community. Find information on all the local farmers' markets located in your area at **www.localharvest.org** and **www.eatwellguide.org**.

2. COMMUNITY-SUPPORTED AGRICULTURE: Another great option for purchasing seasonal foods is joining a community-supported agriculture group in your area. A CSA is a group of consumers who financially agree to support a group of local farmers and share in the benefits and risk of producing the food. Many CSA farmers use organic or biodynamic agriculture for raising their vegetables and fruits. Some CSA's also have local meats, poultry, eggs and dairy available for sale. The weekly cost to receive these local, seasonal foods are very competitively priced because the farmer can go directly to the consumer and keep his or her distribution costs down. By agreeing to pay the farmers early in the season and upfront with your membership, you provide important financial support to these farmers. To find out about local CSAs, go to **www.localharvest.org** and **www.eatwellguide.org**.

3. NATURAL AND HEALTH FOODS MARKETS:

   WHOLE FOODS—Carries a complete variety of whole foods, supplements, and holistic lifestyle products in the United States, Canada, and the United Kingdom. Whole Foods Market is one of my go-to natural food stores to supplement what I get from the farmers' market. They have everything you need to live a holistic lifestyle.

SPROUTS FARMERS MARKET—Carries a great variety of whole foods, supplements, and holistic lifestyle products. Their motto is "healthy living for less." Sprouts Farmers Market is another one of my go-to stores to supplement what I get from the farmers market. Sprouts Farmers Market also carries a large gluten-free product line. Sprouts Farmers Market has 150 stores that are located in Arizona, California, Colorado, Nevada, New Mexico, Oklahoma, Texas, and Utah.

EARTH FARE—Earth Fare is a natural foods store whose mission is to feed and inspire the healthy person inside of you. Earth Fare has 26 stores in Georgia, Kentucky, Indiana, Alabama, North and South Carolina, Ohio, Tennessee, and Florida. Earth Fare carries a complete variety of whole foods, supplements, and holistic lifestyle products at good prices.

TRADER JOE'S—Trader Joe's does not bill itself as a health foods store, but I added them to this list because they do carry a good variety of whole foods, supplements, and holistic lifestyle products at great prices in 300 stores in 35 states in the US. Some of the items they have are organic fresh and frozen fruits and vegetables, wild-caught seafood, gluten-free products, virgin coconut oil, stevia, sprouted breads, raw nuts and seeds, grass-fed meats, organic dairy, and organic eggs.

EREWHON NATURAL FOODS MARKET— Erewhon, which is located in Los Angeles, California, serves as a model store for the natural foods industry, offering a complete and unique variety of whole foods, supplements, homeopathic products, and holistic lifestyle products. They also specialize in offering unique vegan foods and macrobiotic staples. They offer an excellent tonic bar in the store that uses potent superfoods.

LASSEN'S NATURAL FOODS AND VITAMINS—Carries a good variety of whole foods, supplements, and holistic lifestyle products in 11 stores in California. They have a great selection of raw vegan foods, raw dairy, gluten-free products, sprouted breads, inexpensive organic vegetables and fruits from local farmers, cultured vegetables, Kombucha teas, cultured vegetable starter, kefir starter, and healthy beverages.

Tips for Making Healthy Food Preparation Quick and Convenient

1. When shopping please remember to read all food labels and avoid all foods that have a long list of ingredients you can't pronounce or understand. Avoid all chemicals, growth hormones, fillers, preservatives like BHT, BHA, EDTA, THBQ, nitrates, nitrites, MSG, artificial dyes and colors, high fructose corn syrup, artificial sweeteners, and genetically modified ingredients. The best whole foods to buy consist of one or a few unprocessed or minimally processed easily recognized ingredients.

2. Create a grocery list based on the recipes that you want to eat for that week. Pick up what you need at the farmers market or get from your local CSA. Supplement what you find at the farmers market or your CSA with whole foods purchased at your local natural or health foods market or grocery store.

3. Set aside 1 to 2 days per week where you can spend a few hours prepping and preparing foods to eat that following week. You can cut up produce and store it in airtight containers for use later. Lightly wash produce before using with natural vegetable wash or use one part white vinegar and three parts water. Make 2 or 3 salad dressing to last the entire week. Blend organic, unsweetened whole milk or coconut yogurt with healthy sweetener and pure vanilla extract so that it's ready to eat with fresh fruit for a quick, nutritious, tasty breakfast or snack. Make salads like the yuzu cucumber salad, hemp seed herb salad, or beet tartare that will stay fresh for several days. Clean and marinate enough meat or poultry to make for dinner over the next few days.

4. Cut and freeze organic fresh fruit to use in your green energy smoothies, elixirs, tonics, and nut or seed milks. You can also purchase frozen fruit that is already cut if you don't have time to cut your own fruit. Make your own nut or seed milks to use in your smoothies once a week.

TIPS FOR MAKING HEALTHY FOOD PREPARATION QUICK AND CONVENIENT

5. Twice a month set aside time to make batches of cultured vegetables and cultured beverages like coconut kefir. Get your family and friends involved with the preparation. Make enough of these cultured foods to enjoy for the entire month.

6. Buy a slow cooker to make dinner preparation easy. Slow cookers slowly cook food while you are at work or busy doing other things. Slow cookers are great for making soups, meats, and stews. Slow Cookers use less energy than stoves and runs about 2 cents per hour in energy costs on high.

7. Once per week, pre-pack raw or sprouted nuts, seeds, dried fruit, and healthy snack foods in reusable containers so you can grab and go during the week.

8. Be creative with leftovers. For example, lime miso Cornish game hens can be used to top green salads, eaten in sandwiches, or added to homemade soups.

9. Make one pot meals like beef ragu, soups, and mole chili which can be enjoyed for several days or frozen and eaten later on nights when you are too busy to cook.

10. Buy a dehydrator. With a dehydrator you can dehydrate large amounts of seasonal fresh fruits and vegetables, raw vegan snacks, along with soaked nuts and seeds to enjoy in the future. Dehydrators are convenient and easy to use and the Excalibur brand is a good choice.

Pantry Staples for the Holistic Kitchen

The following foods are staples that should be kept on hand to create the recipes in this book.

Fresh fruits, fresh vegetables, pasture-raised meats and poultry, pasture-raised or organic eggs, and raw or organic dairy should be purchased as needed for the recipes you decide to make.

SPROUTED OR RAW NUTS AND SEEDS AND BUTTERS—Choose 2 or more nuts and seeds and nut and seed butters depending on your budget from my list of recommended fats and oils.

COLD OR STONE PRESSED RAW OILS AND BUTTER—My favorite choices: Extra Virgin Olive Oils—O Olive Oil, McEvoy Ranch, California Olive Ranch, Bariani. Avocado Oil—Olivado or Swanson Organic. Extra Virgin Raw Coconut Oil/Butter—Tropical Traditions, Coconut Pacific, Spectrum Organics, Living Tree Community Foods, or Nutiva. Organic Unsalted Sweet and Cultured Butter—Straus Family Creamery, Organic Pastures, Organic Valley, or Humboldt Creamery. Ghee—Purity Farms, Pure Indian Foods. I like to have a good selection of healthy oils/fats on hand. My recipes that use oils/fats list a variety of types you can choose from for each recipe. Choose the oils/fats which suit your taste, health needs, and budget.

CONDIMENTS—Dijon mustard, white miso, organic Ohsawa® Nama® Shoyu soy sauce, or wheat-free Tamari soy sauce, Eden Foods, Spectrum Organics, or Bragg's raw apple cider vinegar. My favorite O vinegars—cassis, pomegranate, yuzu, balsamic, and champagne. Choose the vinegars which suit your taste and budget.

SEA SALT AND ORGANIC SEASONINGS—Celtic or Himalayan small grain sea salt, black peppercorns, cinnamon powder, pure vanilla extract and beans, bay leaves, turmeric powder, cayenne pepper, chipotle powder, green cardamom pods or powder, smoked sweet paprika, Ancho chili powder. Mountain Rose Herbs, Frontier Organics, and Swanson Organics have great organic spices.

NATURAL SWEETENERS—Stevia, coconut (palm) sugar, coconut nectar, raw honey, Rapadura, Sucanat, molasses, organic maple syrup—grade B, lucuma, yacon, or dried unsulfured fruit. Choose 2 or 3 sweeteners which suit your taste, budget, and health needs from this list.

RAW CHOCOLATE (CACAO) AND CAROB—Essential Living Foods, Navitas Naturals, and Vivapura are good for the raw cacao. Foods Alive or Living Tree Community Foods are good for the raw carob.

SPROUTED OR NATURALLY FERMENTED ORGANIC WHOLE GRAINS AND GLUTEN-FREE BREADS—Food For Life, Manna Organics, Grindstone Bakery, or Alvarado Street Bakery.

ORGANIC WHOLE GRAINS AND PASTA—Brown or black rice, buckwheat groats, corn grits, millet, quinoa, brown rice or quinoa pasta, and rolled oats. Choose 3 or 4 from this list which suit your taste and health needs.

ORGANIC BEANS/LEGUMES—Dried black-eyed peas and Eden Foods canned, no-salt-added, organic black beans and garbanzo beans packaged in bisphenol-A-free (BPA-free) cans.

FRESH GARLIC, GINGER, ONIONS, AND HERBS.

RECOMMENDED ONLINE RESOURCES

www.localharvest.org—This site is America's #1 organic and local food Web site. Local Harvest shows you where to find local foods, sustainably grown foods, and organic farmers' markets in your area.

www.organicconsumers.org/—This site is a nonprofit public interest organization campaigning for health, justice, and sustainability. The OCA deals with crucial issues of food safety, industrial agriculture, genetic engineering, children's health, corporate accountability, environmental sustainability, and fair trade.

www.slowfoodusa.org—This site supports good, clean, food that is good to the planet. Slow Food USA® advocates for food and farming policy that is good for the public and good for farmers and workers. I am a member of Slow Food USA®.

www.eatwellguide.org—This site has listings for sustainable, organic, locally grown foods in the United States and Canada.

www.noaa.gov/fishwatch—This site is the lead agency responsible for stewardship of the United States' offshore living marine resources and their habitat. The National Oceanic and Atmospheric Administration (NOAA) fisheries manage, conserve, and protect fish, whales, dolphins, sea turtles, and other ocean creatures. This site has information on sustainable fishing practices and when these fish are in season.

www.montereybayaquarium.org—This site has a seafood watch and downloadable guide for choosing sustainable seafood.

www.seafoodchoices.com—This site has a large database on sustainable fishing practices.

www.ewg.org—This site keeps an updated list of the fruits and vegetables that have the highest levels of toxins and pesticides along with a downloadable produce guide to use. They also have information on cosmetics and household products.

www.eatwild.com—This site lists sources of grass-fed meats and raw diary around the country.

www.cornucopia.org—This site is a nonprofit organic watchdog group.

www.westonaprice.org—This site provides education, activism, and research on the importance of eating nutrient-dense whole foods based on the research conducted by Dr. Weston A. Price.

www.apppa.org—This site has information on pastured poultry producers.

www.assoc.garden.org—The National Gardening Association renews and sustains the essential connection between people, plants, and the environment. They provide free educational plant-based materials, grants, and resources and are the nonprofit leader in plant-based education.

www.aharmonyhealing.com—My site has a holistic blog with healing foods recipes and holistic health tips. We also offer healthy cooking classes, health consultations, radiance wellness parties, corporate health seminars, free product giveaways, Alcat testing, and a holistic supper club.

RECOMMENDED HEALTHY FATS AND OILS

Healthy fats help you feel satisfied, provide naturally occurring vitamins along with essential fatty acids to your body, and are important for maintaining optimum health.

Some of the important roles healthy fats play includes:

- Fat is needed for absorption of the key fat-soluble vitamins A, D, E, and K.
- Fat is an essential component of our cell membranes.
- Fat protects our vital organs and nervous system.
- Fat helps fight systemic inflammation.
- Fat helps contribute to a healthy immune system.
- Fat is a source of energy for the body.

Avoid eating and cooking with highly processed oils like soybean oil, corn oil, cottonseed oil, grapeseed oil, canola oil, margarine, and shortening. These oils are usually chemically extracted, heavily refined, or hydrogenated, along with being subjected to high-heat processing, which destroys many of the oils' important nutrients so that they are no longer healthy fat sources. Some of these oils also can contain genetically modified ingredients. These types of refined oils prevent your body from absorbing the key essential fatty acids that you need for optimum health.

The following list of fats and oils are a better choice for good health. The oils are minimally processed and are extracted gently by cold pressing or stone pressing. These methods of extracting the oil keep the delicate essential fatty acids and beneficial nutrients intact.

Protect healthy oils from exposure to heat, moisture, and light. Store nuts and seeds in the refrigerator. Freeze nuts or seeds for longer storage. Store oils like olive oil in a cool, dark place. Delicate oils like flax, walnut, brazil nut, pumpkin seed, sesame seed, and hemp seed oils should be refrigerated.

Here is the list of healthy fats and oils I recommend adding in moderation to your diet:

SPROUTED OR RAW NUTS, SEEDS, AND BUTTERS FROM NUTS AND SEEDS: Walnuts, Almonds, Pecans, Macadamia Nuts, Brazil Nuts, Pine Nuts, Pistachios, Hazelnuts, Cashews, Sunflower Seeds, Pumpkin Seeds, Flax Seeds, Hemp Seeds, Chia Seeds, Sesame Seeds.

Recommended Brands—Go Raw*, Living Nutz*, Gone Nuts*, Better than Roasted and Love Raw Foods by Blue Mountain Organics*, Living Tree Community Foods*.

Recommended Brands— Vivapura*, Wilderness Family Naturals*, Artisana*, Navitas Naturals*, Nutiva*, Sunfood*, MaraNatha*, Whole Foods, Sprouts, and Trader Joe's private label brands. *companies that have organic raw nuts, seeds, and or butters.

COLD PRESSED OR STONE PRESSED FRUITS OILS: Extra Virgin Olive Oil, Avocado Oil.

Recommended Brands—O Olive Oil, Living Tree Community Foods, California Olive Ranch, McEvoy Ranch, Bariani, Spectrum Organics, Olivado Natural Nutrition, and Swanson Organics.

COLD PRESSED RAW NUT OILS: Coconut, Almond, Walnut, Pistachio, Macadamia Nut, Hazelnut, Brazil Nut.

Recommended Brands—Tropical Traditions, Coconut Pacific, Living Tree Community Foods, Nutiva, Spectrum Organics, Artisana, Jarrow, Radiant Life Company, Living Coconut/The Raw Shoppe, Vivapura, Omega Nutrition, Garden of Life, Olivado Natural Nutrition, Swanson Organics, Essential Living Foods, Trader Joe's private label, and Wilderness Family Naturals.

COLD PRESSED RAW SEED OILS: Pumpkin, Hemp, Flax, Chia, Black and White Sesame.

Recommended Brands—Living Tree Community Foods, Manitoba Harvest, Living Harvest, Nutiva, Eden Foods, Sequel Naturals, Barlean's, Flora Inc., Omega Nutrition, Olivado Natural Nutrition, Foods Alive, and Spectrum Organics.

ORGANIC AND RAW GRASS-FED DAIRY: Goat, Cow, Sheep.

Recommended Brands in California—Organic Pastures*, Claravale Dairy Farm*, Straus Family Creamery, Humboldt Creamery, and Organic Valley. Organic Valley is also located around the United States.

Recommended Brands in other areas in the United States—Larga Vista Ranch*, Hail Family Farms, Stonyfield Farm, Animal Farm, Cedar Summit Dairy, and Green Hills Harvest.

Beyond Organic—Amasai™ cultured dairy beverage, SueroViv™ cultured whey beverage, and raw cow's milk cheese only available online.

Organic Grass-Fed Ghee: Recommended brands—Purity Farms, Pure Indian Foods.

*Raw Milk Dairy Farms

Check out www.realmilk.com for organic dairy farms and creameries in other states.
Beyond Organic can be purchased at: http://shelleyalexander.mybeyondorganic.com

1. STEVIA—Stevia is a natural herb that has been used for centuries to add sweetness to foods and drinks. Green Stevia is the dried leaves that are ground up. Stevia is 300 times sweeter than refined white sugar and does not contain sucrose. Stevia is a safe, plant-based sweetener. Stevia varies in sweetness and taste depending on the company you purchase it from. Make sure you like the taste before you add the stevia to your recipe! Stevia will not raise blood sugar and is safe for diabetics and people who have Candida (yeast). Stevia comes in a whole leaf green powder, a white powder, and a liquid form. Stevia has a glycemic index of 0. Recommended Brands: Navitas Naturals, NuNaturals liquid and pure extract powder, SweetLeaf, Now Foods, and Frontier Organic.

2. COCONUT (PALM) SUGAR/ COCONUT NECTAR—Coconut sugar is the crystallized sap nectar that flows from the coconut blossom when young green coconut trees are tapped. Coconut nectar is the liquid form. Coconut sugar has a delicious taste similar to caramel and has 17 amino acids, key vitamins, and minerals. Coconut sugar and coconut nectar have a low glycemic index of 35. Coconut sugar and coconut nectar are two of the most ecologically sustainable natural sweeteners in the world. Coconut sugar can be used as a 1-to-1 replacement for refined white sugar, and coconut nectar can be used as a 1-to-1 replacement for liquid sweeteners. Both work well in all raw and cooked food applications. Recommended Brands: Wholesome Sweeteners, Essential Living Foods, Coconut Secret, Sweet Tree from Big Tree Farms, Wilderness Family Naturals, and Ultimate Superfoods.

3. RAW HONEY—Raw honey has vitamins, minerals, antioxidants, enzymes, amino acids, and phytonutrients. Recommended Brands: Really Raw Honey, Bee Raw Honey, White Gold Honey, and Wholesome Sweeteners. Children under 1 year of age should not eat raw honey.

4. ORGANIC MAPLE SYRUP/MAPLE SUGAR—Maple syrup is produced by boiling down the sap of maple trees. Maple syrup is a rich source of minerals and comes in different grades. Grade B is my preference due to its rich, full flavor. Maple sugar is produced from removing the water from maple syrup. Maple sugar is crystallized and more expensive than the syrup. Recommended Brands: Coombs Family Farms, Now Foods, and Living Tree Community Foods.

5. **ORGANIC RAPADURA AND SUCANAT**—Rapadura and Sucanat are unrefined, unbleached whole cane sugars that have been dehydrated or naturally evaporated. This process allows the sugar to retain its vitamins and minerals. These sugars can be used in recipes as a 1-to-1 replacement for refined white sugar. Recommended Brands: Rapunzel (Rapadura) and Wholesome Sweeteners (Sucanat).

6. **YACON SYRUP/POWDER/DRIED FRUIT**—Yacon is a natural sweetener from the yacon plant in South America. Yacon is a tuber that tastes like a cross between caramel and molasses. Yacon contains inulin, a complex sugar which breaks down into fructooligosacharide (FOS), a prebiotic which feeds and supports the growth of beneficial bacteria. Yacon is low in calories and contains key vitamins, minerals, and fiber. Yacon is low on the glycemic index and can be used by diabetics because it contains inulin, which passes through the digestive tract undigested. Recommended Brands: Ultimate Superfoods and Navitas Naturals.

7. **LUCUMA**—Lucuma is a fruit from Peru that tastes like a cross between maple and vanilla. Lucuma contains vitamins, minerals, and fiber. Lucuma has a low glycemic index and is low in calories. Recommended Brands: Vivapura, Ultimate Superfoods, Essential Living Foods, and Navitas Naturals.

8. **UNSULFURED UNSWEETENED DRIED FRUIT**—Dried dates, figs, raisins, goji berries, and any dried fruit can be used as a natural sweetener. Dried fruits are a good source of vitamins, minerals, and fiber. The natural sugars in dried fruit are much more concentrated, so use in moderation for people watching their sugar intake.

9. **UNSULFURED ORGANIC BLACKSTRAP MOLASSES**—Blackstrap molasses is made from repeated boiling of raw sugarcane. Blackstrap molasses is a good source of iron, calcium, potassium, and B vitamins. Recommended Brand: Wholesome Sweeteners.

FLAVOR ENHANCERS WITH HEALTH ADVANTAGES

Flavor enhancers are sea salts, herbs, spices, rhizomes, fruit pods, and vegetables, which really enhance and elevate the flavor in my recipes. The 22 flavor enhancers I use have important health benefits that will aid your body's own natural healing abilities. Feel free to experiment with them to find out which ones are your favorites.

1. Celtic Sea Salt—Celtic sea salt is a natural moist sea salt harvested from Brittany, France, which contains a great balance of key trace minerals. Celtic sea salt has a light grey color and clean flavor, with no additives of any kind. It enhances any foods that you add it to. Celtic sea salt comes in coarse or fine grain texture. The brands of Celtic sea salt that I use are Vital Mineral Blend from The Grain and Salt Society, Eden Foods, and Gold Mine Natural Food Company. It is important for your health to use moderate amounts of any salt, including unrefined sea salt.

2. Himalayan Sea Salt—Himalayan sea salt is an ancient crystal sea salt from the Himalayan mountains that contains 84 key trace minerals. Himalayan sea salt has no additives of any kind and has a clean flavor and beautiful pink color. It imparts an amazing taste to any foods that you add it to. This sea salt is my first choice for recipes. Himalayan sea salt comes in blocks, slabs, and coarse, medium, or small grain. The brands I use are the small-grain version by Foods Alive, Aloha Bay, Essential Living Foods, or Salt Works. It is important for your health to use moderate amounts of any salt, including unrefined sea salt.

3. Garlic—Garlic is an allium vegetable and member of the Lily family. Garlic adds aromatic flavor to foods and is used in a variety of ways, including whole, sliced, chopped, minced, crushed, or dried. Roasting garlic makes the flavor milder. Garlic is high in Vitamin C and B6 and is an immune system booster. Garlic also contains key minerals like iron, potassium, and sulfur, along with 70 active phytochemicals, including allicin. Garlic is a potent anti-microbial and has been shown to lower total serum cholesterol, and lower blood pressure.

4. Mint—Mint is one of the most common used herbs in history. Members of the mint family include peppermint, spearmint, rosemary, basil, sage, thyme, oregano, savory, and lemon balm. Mint has a wide variety of health benefits for our bodies. Mint contains key phytochemicals which are strong cancer fighters. Mint is also a commonly used digestive aid.

5. Parsley—Parsley is an herb that comes in curly or flat leaf. Parsley contains carotenes, chlorophyll, vitamin C, calcium, iron, potassium, and fiber. Parsley helps purify the blood, helps protect the body against cancer, and is an excellent digestive aid.

6. Turmeric—Turmeric is a rhizome that is a member of the ginger family. Turmeric is available as a fresh root or dried and ground into powder. Turmeric contains the active ingredient curcumin, which is a potent antioxidant, liver supporter, blood purifier, and good anti-inflammatory.

7. Sweet Basil—Sweet basil is an herb that comes from an annual green plant that is a member of the mint family. There are over 60 varieties of basil with sweet basil being the most common. Basil can be used fresh, dried, ground, or as an essential oil. Basil has important cancer fighting flavonoids and carotenes that protect the body from free radicals. Basil helps restore balance in the body, is great for digestive disorders, and has been used to fight intestinal parasites. Basil contains the essential oil eugenol which functions as an anti-inflammatory.

8. Cilantro/Coriander—Cilantro is the leaves of the coriander plant a member of the carrot family and is treated as both an herb and a spice because both the green leaves and the seeds are used. Cilantro leaves have a distinct earthy taste and the coriander seeds have a citrus taste. Cilantro and coriander have been shown to have a variety of benefits for the body including fighting inflammation, chelating or pulling heavy metals, yeasts, and fungus from the body, and aiding digestion.

9. Tarragon—Tarragon is an herb with a sweet aromatic flavor that has a taste similar to anise or fennel. Tarragon comes in 2 varieties including French and Russian tarragon. I prefer French tarragon because it has more essential oil and a sweeter taste than the Russian tarragon. Tarragon is a digestive aid, is high in natural antioxidants, and has anti-microbial properties because of the compound estragol which is contained in the essential oil.

10. Ginger—Ginger is a rhizome which can be eaten fresh, dried, ground, crystallized, preserved, and pickled. Ginger has traditionally been used as a digestive aid because of its ability to relax and calm the intestinal tract. Ginger also stimulates bile flow from the gallbladder. Ginger contains high amounts of potassium and has been used to relieve nausea, decrease inflammation, and increase circulation. Ginger has a slightly spicy flavor.

11. Cinnamon—Cinnamon is from the inner bark of an evergreen tree. Cinnamon can be used to enhance savory or sweet dishes. Cinnamon is available in ground form or sticks and adds a unique and recognizable aromatic flavor to whatever foods you use it with. Cinnamon comes in different varieties, with Ceylon or Cassia being two of the most popular. Ceylon, a.k.a. true cinnamon is my favorite choice due its wonderful sweet, mild taste. Cinnamon contains iron and calcium and has a multitude of health benefits for the body, such as stabilization of blood sugar.

12. Vanilla Beans—Vanilla beans are the fruit pods of an orchid that adds a unique, warm, floral flavor and perfumed aroma to any recipe they are used in. Tahitian or Madagascar vanilla beans, powder, and extract are my personal favorites. If you use the extract, make sure that it says pure vanilla extract and not imitation vanilla. Vanilla is an excellent digestive aid.

13. Thyme—Thyme is a member of the mint family. Thyme contains the essential oil thymol, which is used as an antiseptic and antibacterial in many different products. Thyme is high in antioxidants, which help to strengthen the immune system and fight free radicals.

14. Black Peppercorns—Black peppercorns are one of the most popular seasoning in the world. Peppercorns are the dried black berries from the vine pepper. Peppercorns add a unique pungent flavor to many dishes and help to enhance the flavor of other ingredients. Black peppercorns should be freshly ground to bring out the best flavor and aroma. Black peppercorns contain piperine which has been shown to have a thermogenic fat burning effect on the body as well as an aid to help detoxify the liver. Black peppercorns stimulate our taste buds and hydrochloric acid production which aid in improving digestion.

15. Star Anise—Star Anise is the dried fruit of an evergreen from China. Star Anise has a licorice flavor and contains the essential oil anethole which aids digestion. Anise is also great for clearing up respiratory disorders like coughs and excess mucus.

16. Cayenne—Cayenne or red pepper is the fruit from a tropical plant called the capsicum annuum longum. Cayenne pepper is high in nutrients including carotenes and vitamin C. Cayenne has a high amount of capsaicin which is a proven pain reliever, fat burner, digestive aid, metabolism booster, and cardiovascular aid. If on warfarin, antacids, or aspirin consult a doctor before eating.

17. Cardamom— Cardamom is an ancient spice from a fruit that contains up to 18 seeds and is native to Tanzania, Malaysia, and Sri Lanka. Cardamom seeds have a flavor similar to ginger and are a great digestive aid for gas and indigestion. The green and white cardamom pods have great floral flavor, essential oils, and aroma and are considered an aphrodisiac.

18. **Smoked Spanish paprika**—Smoked paprika or Pimentón de la Vera is red capsicum pepper that is smoked, dried, and ground. Smoked sweet paprika has a sweet, smoky flavor. Smoked hot paprika is spicier. Paprika is good for blood pressure regulation, and is high in antioxidants like vitamin C. Paprika is also noted for its antibacterial properties.

19. **Wasabi**—Wasabi is a rhizome or root from Japan that is a member of the cruciferous family of vegetables and is traditionally used to enhance sushi and sashimi. True wasabi has a spicy flavor and is called wasabia japonica. Fresh true wasabi is grated for use. Wasabi contains potassium, magnesium, vitamin C, and calcium.

20. **Oregano**—Oregano is an herb in the mint family and has one of the highest amounts of antioxidants of any herb, fruit, and vegetable. Oregano also has strong anti-microbial properties.

21. **Cumin**—Cumin is the seed of an herb from the parsley family that has a musky flavor that is used extensively in the cuisines of India, Mexico, China, and Africa. Cumin helps protect the body against free radicals, aids liver function, has antibacterial properties, and is a potent digestive aid.

22. **Dill**—Dill is a popular herb that is great for liver detoxification and digestive disorders. Dill contains flavonoids and has anti-microbial and anti-cancer benefits.

HEALTHY PREPARED FOODS OPTIONS

The following list has some great prepared whole foods that are a convenient healthy option to replace unhealthy junk foods. I have personally tasted these foods and feel confident about recommending them.

1. Go Raw—Go Raw has some amazing organic, gluten-free, vegan, raw, sprouted bars, flax snaxs, super chips, super cookies, sprouted granola, and sprouted seeds that have been dehydrated at low temperatures. I can't resist their sprouted pumpkin seeds, sprouted super cookies, sprouted granola, and sprouted spicy seed mix. You can purchase their products in health food stores and online at www.goraw.com.

2. Vivapura—Vivapura has some of the best organic, raw vegan trail mixes, raw nut butters, dried fruits, spirulina crunchies, and coconut crèmes. I also enjoy their jakfruit, salad mix, sun-dried Botija olives, chia seeds, and bee pollen. You can purchase Vivapura products in health food stores and online at www.vivapura.com, or at www.aharmonyhealing.com.

3. Essential Living Foods—ELF has a wide range of delectable, organic, fair-trade products, including truly raw cacao powder, coconut sugar, trail mix, smoothie mixes, maca root, chia seeds, goji berries, sun-dried olives, and chocolate kits. You can purchase their products in health food stores and online at www.essentiallivingfoods.com, or at www.aharmonyhealing.com.

4. Wilderness Family Naturals—WFN has a wide variety of delicious organic products, including coconut sugar, coconut milk, coconut oil, coconut vinegar, coconut water, sprouted nuts, sprouted seeds, black rice, mayonnaise, salad dressings, raw chocolate, and dried fruit. You can purchase their products online at www.wildernessfamilynaturals.com.

5. Blue Mountain Organics—Blue Mountain Organics makes fabulous sprouted nuts, seeds and butters, love bites, sprouted cereals, sprouted grains, sprouted flours, and raw vegan superfood snacks. You can purchase their products in health food stores and online at www.bluemountainorganics.com.

6. Gone Nuts/Living Intentions—Gone Nuts /Living Intentions have a variety of mouthwatering organic, sprouted, and low-temperature dehydrated nuts and seeds in flavors like cilantro lime, mesquite maple, rosemary garlic, and sun-dried tomato marinara. They also make delicious gluten-free cereals, sprouted flours, and salad toppings. You can purchase Gone Nuts and Living Intention products in health food stores and online at www.livingintentions.com.

7. Living Tree Community Foods—Living Tree Community Foods has a wide variety of unique, delectable, organic foods including raw almond butter, raw cashew butter, raw tahini, raw pistachio butter, raw walnut butter, raw chocolate ecstasy, raw chia seed oil, raw black sesame oil, dried fruits, baby quinoa, coconut products, raw nuts, raw seeds, and whole grains. You can purchase their products in health food stores and online at www.livingtreecommunity.com.

8. Lydia's Organics—Lydia's Organics makes delicious raw, organic, gluten-free, vegan foods including sprouted crackers, breads, fruit bars, and grain-less cereals. You can purchase Lydia's Organics in health food stores and online at www.lydiasorganics.com.

9. Foods Alive—Foods Alive makes wonderful organic, kosher, raw vegan foods including eight varieties of dehydrated flax crackers, artisan cold-pressed flax, hemp, black sesame, and chia seed oils, healthy salad dressings, hemp foods, chia seeds, plus many other superfoods. You can purchase Foods Alive in health food stores and online at www.foodsalive.com.

Unique Superfoods for Energy, Strength, and Immunity

These unique superfoods are an easy way to add more high quality nutrition into your life. Descriptions of these superfoods and their benefits are included throughout the book. I have personally tried these superfoods and have had great success and experienced great improvement in my health by incorporating them into my diet. If you are on a budget, I recommend you eat cultured foods regularly and buy digestive plant enzymes and essential fatty acids supplements to take on a daily basis. This cookbook has recipes to make your own inexpensive cultured vegetables, cultured salsa, cultured fruit compote, and coconut kefir.

- **Cultured/Fermented Foods**
  Recommended Brands—Rejuvenative Foods, Glaser Organic Farms, Immunitrition, Zukay Live Foods, Gold Mine Natural Food Company, and Healing Movement.

- **Greens and Fruits Superfood Powders and Raw Protein Powders**
  Recommended Brands—Garden of Life, Amazing Grass, Navitas Naturals, HealthForce Nutritionals, Vega, VitaForce, Essential Living Foods, and Boku.

- **Plant-Based Digestive Enzymes and Probiotics**
  Recommended Brands—Garden of Life, Digest All by MRM, HealthForce Nutritionals Digestion Enhancement Enzymes, New Chapter Organics Probiotic Immunity, Prescript Assist, Jarrow, and Dr. Ohhira's Probiotics.

- **Blue Green Algae, Spirulina, Chlorella**
  Recommended Brands—E3 Live, Green Tara, Vivapura, HealthForce Nutritionals, Sun Chlorella, and Sunfood.

Unique Superfoods for Energy, Strength, and Immunity

🦋 Hemp Seeds and Hemp Protein Powder

Recommended Brands—Manitoba Harvest, Living Harvest, Nutiva, Vivapura, HealthForce Nutritionals, and Navitas Naturals.

🦋 Coconut Water, Coconut Milk, Coconut Kefir

Recommended Brands—Coconut Water: Harmless Harvest, Vita Coco, Harvest Bay, Body Ecology, Wilderness Family Naturals, and One.

Coconut Milk: Native Forest, Thai Kitchen Organic, Wilderness Family Naturals, Dabur, and Whole Foods Market brand.

Coconut Kefir: Body Ecology, Kevita, Living Coconut, and Healing Movement.

🦋 Essential Fatty Acids Supplements

Recommended Brands—Minami Nutrition, Nordic Naturals, New Chapter, Barlean's, Carlson Labs, Doctor's Best, Garden of Life, and Dr. Ohhira's.

🦋 Chia Seeds

Recommended Brands—Living Tree Community Foods and Foods Alive.

HEALTHY BEVERAGES TO GET THE GLOW

I love to create my own healing beverages, like cultured coconut kefir and green energy smoothies, that help you get the glow of good health and don't deplete your health like beverages filled with artificial sweeteners, refined white sugar, high fructose corn syrup, chemicals, artificial flavors, and other ingredients that don't promote vibrant health.

I use many of the following beverages on a daily basis when I want something that is quick, healthy, convenient, and delicious! Try the following brands and decide which ones are your favorites.

1. **Herbal, White, Green, and Black teas**
   Recommended Brands—Zhena's Gypsy Tea, Republic of Tea, Yogi Tea, Mountain Rose Herbs, Numi Tea, Organic India, Two Leaves and a Bud, Eden Foods, Pukka Herbs, Good Nature, Choice Organics, Stash Organics, Teavana Tea, Teas' unsweetened tea by Ito En, and Steaz unsweetened ice tea.

2. **Coconut Kefir, Whey, and Cultured Dairy Beverages**
   Recommended Brands—Kevita, Body Ecology, Healing Movement, and Living Coconut. Amasai™ cultured dairy beverage, and SueroViv™ cultured whey beverage from Beyond Organic*.

3. **Herbal Coffee**
   Recommended Brands—Teeccino and Dandy Blend.

4. **Coconut Water**
   Recommended Brands—Harmless Harvest, Vita Coco, One, Body Ecology, Wilderness Family Naturals, and Harvest Bay.

5. **Kombucha Tea**
   Recommended Brands—GT Synergy, High Country, and Katalyst Kombucha.

*Beyond Organic products are only sold online by mission marketers. Find these products at http://shelleyalexander.mybeyondorganic.com

SMOKE POINT OF OILS FOR COOKING

When cooking with heat and oil, it is very important to know the smoke point of oils. Once you pass the smoke point of any oil, it starts smoking and begins to become unstable, break down, release carcinogens, release trans fats, and change its chemical composition.

Oil that has gone over its smoke point and broken down is not healthy for you to eat. Never heat oil past its smoke point, and always discard oil if it starts smoking.

Another important consideration when cooking with oils is the fatty acid profile. Oils that have higher amounts of saturated fats are more stable when cooking with heat.

Extra Virgin Cold or Stone Pressed Olive Oil—up to 350° F. Good for moderate temperature cooking and for cold use.

Cold Pressed Avocado Oil—up to 500° F. Good for moderate temperature cooking and for cold use.

Organic Clarified Butter or Ghee—up to 485° F. Good for high temperature cooking.

Raw Virgin Coconut Oil—up to 350° F. Good for moderate temperature cooking.

Organic Unsalted Butter—up to 350° F. Good for moderate temperature cooking.

Cold Pressed Macadamia Nut Oil—up to 450° F. Good for low temperature cooking and for cold use.

Cold Pressed Red Palm Oil—up to 450° F. Good for high temperature cooking.

KITCHEN EQUIPMENT

This list includes some of my favorite equipment for being efficient in the kitchen. Only buy what you need and can afford. The top pieces of kitchen equipment that I use daily are my Blendtec blender, chefs' knives, cutting boards, cast iron skillet, saucepans, and baking pan.

Knives—Knives are important for doing all types of cutting, dicing, and chopping. Always make sure you keep your knives sharp and use them correctly to avoid accidents. Use a steel to keep your knife edges honed. My favorite knives are the 8-inch or 10-inch chef's knife, 4-inch paring knife, and 8-inch serrated knife. Some brands I recommend are Global, Henckels, and Kyocera ceramic knives.

Blender—A high-speed, powerful blender is essential for many kitchen tasks. A Blendtec blender is the one I currently own, love, and personally use on a daily basis. It's easy to use, has a lot of horsepower, is computerized, easy to clean, lightweight, and great for any blending task you give it. You can purchase Blendtec on their site or on my Web site by clicking on the Blendtec link. The other high-speed blender I recommend and have used is Vitamix. I grew up using the Vitamix blender at home and when working in commercial kitchens. Both blenders are very efficient and reliable.

Food Processor—The food processor is one of the best multitask items you can have in your kitchen. It is easy to use and clean. Cuisinart and Breville both have efficient and powerful food processors.

Mandoline—Mandolines are wonderful and highly effective for slicing evenly and making different types of cuts, like julienne. A ceramic Mandoline is good and costs less than a steel Mandoline. Make sure to always use the guard when slicing to protect your fingers from injury.

Hand or Immersion Blender—A hand blender can perform many tasks such as blending hot soups or sauces in the pot and is a good option if you want something economical and convenient.

Skillet and Sauté Pan—A 10-inch and 12-inch skillet and sauté pan are very versatile pans for most recipes. Cast iron is my top choice for skillets or sauté pans. I'm a happy owner of both Lodge and Le Creuset cast iron cookware and I recommend them both. Both companies make durable, high performance, top quality cookware. Lodge's cookware comes in preseasoned iron and enameled cast iron. Le Creuset's cookware comes in enameled cast iron. Follow the care instructions listed on the website for the brand you purchase.

Saucepans with Lids—A variety of saucepans are convenient for making soups, sauces, and many other foods. Saucepans are available in many sizes and are good for cooking on top of the stove. 1½-quart and 3-quart sizes are versatile and good to own.

Stockpot—A large pot used to cook stocks and soups. Stockpots are available in a variety of quart sizes. I use a large stainless steel stockpot to make all of my stocks.

Glass Mason Jars—Glass jars in 8-ounce, 16-ounce, and 1- or 2-quart sizes are good for storing dressings, cultured vegetables, nut and seed milks, and grains. I prefer the wide-mouth varieties.

Salad Spinner—Great for cleaning and drying leafy greens and herbs. My favorite brand is OXO.

Microplane—The Microplane is an invaluable rasp-like grater for creating fine zest from citrus fruits and for grating garlic, hard cheeses, ginger, chocolate, onions, and shallots.

Cutting Boards—Cutting boards are used in conjunction with your knife to cut a variety of food products. It is very important to avoid cross contamination of your food. I prefer to have clearly marked, separate cutting boards for produce and meats. The cutting board should be thoroughly cleaned and sanitized with eco-friendly, safe cleaners after use. Cutting boards are available in wood, plastic, and hard rubber.

Slow Cooker—Slow cookers cook food at low temperatures in a ceramic crock. I recommend the Crock-Pot by Rival. Slow Cookers use less energy than stoves and runs about 2 cents per hour in energy costs on high.

Ice Cream Maker—A good ice cream maker will make fresh, homemade ice cream in minutes without preservatives, corn syrup, artificial flavors, and fillers. I recommend the Cuisinart ice cream maker because of the ease of use, convenience, reliability, and low cost.

Sheet Pans—Sheet pans are rectangular pans with shallow sides that are ideal for baking. Sheet pans are available in half or full size. Half size fits in most home ovens.

Mixing Bowls—Round bowls are used for mixing a variety of different foods. My personal favorites are made of glass or stainless steel.

Measuring Cups/Measuring Spoons—Measuring cups are used to measure dry or liquid ingredients. I use glass for liquids and stainless steel for dry ingredients. Measuring spoons are used to measure small amounts of ingredients like dry spices, sea salt, and natural sweeteners.

Spatula—A utensil used to flip, turn, fold, mix, scrape, and lift a variety of foods in bowls, pots, or pans. Spatulas are available in rubber, silicone, wood, stainless steel, and plastic.

Kitchen Equipment

Large Spoons—Large spoons are perfect for mixing, stirring, and serving food. My favorite spoons are made of wood or stainless steel, and I use both solid and perforated spoons.

Vegetable Peeler—Good for removing skin from vegetables and fruits. My favorite brand for soft skin fruit is from Zyliss. The Zyliss regular peeler is good for vegetables.

Electric Spice Grinder—A spice grinder is great for grinding fresh whole spices into powders.

Nut Milk Bag—Nut milk bags are inexpensive bags that are used for straining nut or seed pulp from homemade nut or seed milks. Amazon has nut bags for sell. Use the pulp in other recipes.

Chinois and China Caps—These are types of strainers shaped like a cone that are used for straining liquids, sauces, stocks, and soups. Chinois have very fine mesh for creating extremely smooth foods. A regular round, fine-mesh basket strainer is an inexpensive option to the Chinois or China Cap.

Important Note about Fresh Fruits and Vegetables

Many of my recipes feature fresh, locally grown, organic, seasonal fruits and vegetables in their natural, raw state. Fresh fruits and vegetables can vary in water content, sweetness, tartness, texture, etc., depending on the time of season when the produce is harvested, level of ripeness when picked, growing conditions, and how long you store the produce. This may affect my recipes slightly, so they may not have exactly the same taste each time that you prepare them. For example, a tomato may vary in taste from sweet to slightly acidic, so you may need to adjust my recipes slightly. I love this small variation and feel that it keeps your foods interesting and exciting for your palate. Let your own taste buds be your guide, and feel free to slightly adjust my recipes to suit your personal tastes. To find out what fruits and vegetables are in season in your local area, check out www.localharvest.org or www.sustainabletable.org.

IMPORTANT TIPS FOR IMPROVING YOUR DIGESTIVE HEALTH

1. Do 2–3 minutes of deep breathing to relax before eating your meal. Eating in a relaxed state will help you digest your food more efficiently.

2. Enjoy 8 ounces or more of cultured or fermented probiotic and enzyme-rich beverages like Kombucha tea, coconut kefir, cultured whey, or beet kvass daily to aid digestion.

3. Drink spring or filtered water during the course of the day with a squeeze of alkalizing lemon juice. Add a pinch of Celtic or Himalayan sea salt or drops of Cellfood® if drinking reverse osmosis water to replace the minerals that have been removed. Avoid drinking water during your meals, which can dilute your digestive power.

4. Savor your meal and take time to enjoy each bite and all the wonderful flavors, aromas, and textures you are experiencing making sure to thoroughly chew your food. Digestion starts in the mouth, so take your time!

5. Eat cultured or fermented vegetables and fruits on a daily basis to help boost your digestive power and provide your body with healthy probiotics and enzymes.

6. Take probiotic pills on a daily basis, especially if you have digestive issues and don't eat enough probiotic-rich foods. Good choices for probiotics are Raw Probiotics or Primal Defense® Ultra by Garden of Life, Jarrow, New Chapter Organics Probiotic Immunity, Prescript Assist by Safer Medical Inc., or Dr. Ohhira's Probiotics.

7. Take plant-based digestive enzymes with each meal to give your digestion additional enzyme support. Good choices are Garden of Life Raw Enzymes, MRM Digest All, and HealthForce Nutritionals Digestion Enhancement Enzymes.

8. Take regular time out of each day to eliminate stool. Never ignore the natural urge to go to the bathroom, and relax during the process.

9. Drink green energy smoothies on a regular basis to help you obtain a good amount of fresh fruits, vegetables, water, chlorophyll, and fiber in a way that is easy for your body to absorb and to digest the nutrients.

SEASONAL MENUS

FALL MENU 1

Breakfast

Rainbow Chard Omelet

Cultured Probiotic Vegetables

Snack

Green Energy Smoothie

Lunch

Portobello Mushroom and Grilled Onion Burger

Chicken Coconut Soup

Cultured Probiotic Vegetables

Snack

Broccoli Florets, Endive, and Organic Celery

Aged Balsamic Vinaigrette

Dinner

Arugula Comice Pear Salad

3-Herb Pesto Wild Halibut

Potato Parsley Mash

Cultured Probiotic Vegetables

FALL MENU 2

Breakfast

Green Energy Smoothie

Snack

Cinnamon Almond Coconut Kefir

Sprouted or Raw Pumpkin Seeds

Lunch

Chicken Vegetable Quinoa Salad

Sweet Potato Maple Soup

Cultured Probiotic Vegetables

Snack

Hazelnut Herbal Coffee

Sprouted or Raw Walnut or Hemp Seed Butter

Organic Pear Slices

Dinner

Red Cabbage Apple Salad

Mole Chili

Cultured Probiotic Vegetables

SEASONAL MENUS

WINTER MENU 1

Breakfast

Caramelized Balsamic Onion Scramble

Cultured Probiotic Vegetables

Snack

Green Energy Smoothie

Lunch

Baby Spinach, Ambrosia Apple, and Blood Orange Salad

Pumpkin Hazelnut Chai Soup

Snack

Vanilla Cardamom Coconut Kefir

Raw Brazil Nuts

Dinner

Lime Miso Cornish Game Hens

Garlic Collard Greens

Slow-Cooked Black-Eyed Peas

Green Onions

Cultured Probiotic Vegetables

SEASONAL MENUS

WINTER MENU 2

Breakfast

Chai Pumpkin Oatmeal

Cultured Apple Goji Berry Compote

Snack

Chive Deviled Eggs

Lunch

Smoky Orange Hummus with Sprouted Flax Seed Crackers

Organic Romaine Salad with Olives and Carrot Tahini Dressing

Roasted Winter Vegetables

Snack

Manna Organics Sprouted Carrot Raisin Bread

Spiced Milk Tea Tonic

Dinner

Lamb Chops with Spicy Mint Chutney

Purple Cauliflower Mash

Pomegranate Millet Pilaf

Cultured Probiotic Vegetables

SPRING MENU 1

Breakfast

Green Energy Smoothie

Snack

Spicy Guacamole

Organic Carrot Sticks and Asparagus

Lunch

Mixed Baby Greens Salad

Wild Salmon Vegetable Sushi Rolls

Snack

Pineapple Coconut Kefir

Sprouted or Raw Walnuts

Dinner

Organic Red Oak Leaf Lettuce Salad

Lemon Herb Wild Black Cod

Shitake Mushroom Sauté

Steamed Quinoa

Cultured Probiotic Vegetables

SEASONAL MENUS

SPRING MENU 2

Breakfast

Buttermilk Millet Waffles

Fresh Organic Strawberries

Soft Boiled Egg

Snack

Green Energy Smoothie

Lunch

Lemon Ginger Tulsi Tea

Mixed Vegetable Pea Shoots Sandwich

Snack

Encrusted Goat Cheese

Organic Celery Sticks

Dinner

Organic Butter Lettuce Salad

Beef Ragu over Quinoa Pasta or Brown Rice Pasta

Roasted Lemon Fennel and Onions

Cultured Probiotic Vegetables

SEASONAL MENUS

SUMMER MENU 1

Breakfast
Green Energy Smoothie

Snack
Carrot Orange Tonic

Sprouted or Raw Sunflower Seeds

Lunch
Italian Vegetable Salad with Black Pepper Croutons

Raw Watermelon Jicama Soup

Snack
Carob Almond Chia Pudding

Dinner
Micro Greens Salad

Lemongrass Ginger Wild Salmon

Zucchini Onion Sauté

Brown Rice Pilaf

Cultured Probiotic Vegetables

SUMMER MENU 2

Breakfast

Green Energy Smoothie

Snack

Berries and Cream

Lunch

Sardine Lettuce Wraps

Raw Corn Chowder

Snack

Peach Lemonade Elixir

Pumpkin Seed Spread

Sprouted Flax Seed Crackers

Dinner

Lemon Cucumber and Sweet Bell Pepper Salad

Dijon Honey Chicken Wings

Basil Garlic Spinach

Black Rice Pilaf

Cultured Probiotic Vegetables

ESSENTIAL BASICS

ESSENTIAL BASICS ARE RECIPES THAT ARE USED IN A VARIETY OF OTHER RECIPES THROUGHOUT THE BOOK. FEEL FREE TO USE THEM IN SOME OF YOUR FAVORITE PERSONAL RECIPES AS WELL.

OVEN-DRIED TOMATOES

BLOOD ORANGE COCONUT BUTTER

SPICED MAPLE SYRUP

Yields around 1 cup

THIS SPICED MAPLE SYRUP is good on hot cereal, in yogurt, smoothies, mixed in nut butter, and on French toast. The spices and vanilla add a warm flavor and mild spice note that elevates the maple syrup.

1 cup organic maple syrup—grade B

1 teaspoon orange zest

1 cinnamon stick

3 black peppercorns

Seeds from 1 vanilla bean or 1 tablespoon pure vanilla extract

Mix all ingredients in small saucepan and cook over low heat for 15–20 minutes to allow flavors to meld, stirring occasionally. Store spiced maple syrup in a glass jar with a lid in the refrigerator.

CLARIFIED BUTTER

Yields around 1¾ cups

CLARIFIED BUTTER is butter that does not contain milk solids. The milk solids are removed and only the butterfat is left. This butterfat is excellent to use for high temperature cooking because it has a smoke point of 485° F. I use unsalted butters like Straus Family Creamery or Humboldt Creamery to make the clarified butter. Clarified butter is a simple butter to make at home and lasts for 2 months at room temperature or 4–6 months in the refrigerator. If you want to make ghee, cook butter until milk solids turn golden brown and smell nutty, being careful not to burn butter.

16 ounces organic unsalted butter, cut in large cubes

Slowly heat the butter in a small saucepan over low heat. Do not stir the butter! Once the butter melts, remove from the heat and skim the foam off the top of the butter with a large spoon and throw foam away. The clarified butter will be golden in color, and the milk solids are cloudy and milky and will be at the bottom of the saucepan. Place a thin towel or doubled cheesecloth on top of a wide-mouth jar and carefully pour the golden clarified butter into the jar while holding the towel or cheesecloth, making sure you leave the milk solids in the bottom of the pan. Throw the milk solids away. Cover the jar with a lid and store clarified butter in the refrigerator or at room temperature.

CULTURED PROBIOTIC VEGETABLES

Yields (4) 1-Quart jars

CULTURED OR FERMENTED VEGETABLES are something you should enjoy daily to keep your digestive system healthy and filled with probiotics, the good bacteria. This recipe is my go-to basic recipe, but feel free to experiment with any combination of vegetables and herbs that you like.

4 stalks organic celery—cut in half

2 organic Persian cucumbers—cut in half

1 small organic apple—unpeeled, cored, and seeded

1 packet vegetable culture starter or ½ cup liquid whey (recipe on page 64)

2 large organic green cabbage heads—reserve 8 outer leaves for placing in jars

4–5 peeled organic carrots

3 cups filtered or spring water (warm to 90° F)

1 tablespoon unrefined sea salt

2-inch piece fresh peeled ginger—grated

4 clean 1-quart, large-mouth, glass mason jars with lids

Clean and rinse all produce thoroughly and set aside. In blender, place celery, cucumbers, apple, and 3 cups of water and blend into liquid. Add more water if liquid is too thick. Stir in culture starter by hand and allow mixture to sit for 20 minutes at room temperature to allow the good bacteria to wake up and feed on the sugars from the apple and vegetables. Skip this step if using whey. Cut cabbage heads into wedges, remove core, and place wedges into a food processor fitted with the shredder blade attachment and shred. Place cabbage into a large bowl. Next shred carrots in food processor and add to the bowl. Stir sea salt and ginger into cabbage-carrot mixture and mix well with your clean hands. Once liquid has set for 20 minutes, pour on top of cabbage mixture and mix well to ensure that all the vegetables are coated with this brine. Add whey at this point if using in place of culture starter. Place vegetables in clean, dry jars and pack down firmly with your fist to remove air. Make sure vegetables are covered with brine. Fill the jars and allow 2 inches at the top of the jar for vegetables to expand. Fold reserved cabbage leaves and place 2 leaves inside each jar, pressing down to submerge cultured vegetables under the brine. Wipe off the mouth of each jar and place lid on vegetables. Ferment vegetables at room temperature away from light for at least 5–7 days. The longer the vegetables ferment the more tangy they will taste. Refrigerate once vegetables have cultured to taste. Vegetables will last for 4–6 months in the refrigerator. Each time you remove vegetables, use a spoon to push remaining vegetables under the brine so they stay fresh. ⌒

*Raw Vegan

OVEN-DRIED TOMATOES

Makes around 4 cups

OVEN-DRIED TOMATOES are a great way to preserve large amounts of fresh tomatoes when they are in their peak season. I love to eat them as a snack or use in a variety of different recipes to add additional nutrients, flavor, and texture. Oven-dried tomatoes have a sweet flavor and chewy texture that is wonderful. Experiment with different varieties of tomatoes to discover your favorite.

10–12 small heirloom or roma tomatoes

2 tablespoons extra virgin olive oil or melted virgin coconut oil

1 teaspoon coconut sugar or Rapadura—optional

¼ teaspoon unrefined sea salt

Preheat oven to 250° F. Line a sheet pan with parchment paper or a silicone mat and set aside. Remove green tops from the tomatoes and cut into ½-inch slices. In large bowl blend together olive or coconut oil, sweetener, and sea salt. Add tomato slices and toss lightly to coat completely with the oil. Put tomatoes on sheet pan and bake for 3–5 hours until tomatoes have dried and shriveled down in size. Remove from oven and cool completely before storing in covered containers. Tomatoes will last for around 21 days at room temperature. Tomatoes will last for 2 months if covered with olive oil and refrigerated. If you own a dehydrator, you can place tomatoes on teflex sheets on the dehydrator trays and dehydrate tomatoes at 115° F until dried and chewy. ⌒

*Vegan

I CREATED THESE COCONUT-OLIVE OIL BLENDS for anyone who doesn't eat butter. The olive oils are cold pressed with organic fruits and have an intense flavor that blends beautifully with the raw virgin coconut oil. Raw virgin coconut oil is one of my favorite healthy fats. Coconuts contain high amounts of lauric acid and capric acid, which are key fatty acids that have antibacterial, anti-viral, and anti-microbial properties. These medium chain fatty acids are used for energy production and are easier for your body to digest. These oils are wonderful to use in a variety of different recipes. Once you refrigerate the oils, they solidify and have a pretty yellow color and can be used in recipes as a substitute for real butter. I made my favorites, but feel free to experiment with different flavors of cold pressed oils with fruits or raw nut or seed oils.

BLOOD ORANGE COCONUT BUTTER

Yields ½ cup

¼ cup O blood orange extra virgin olive oil

¼ cup melted virgin coconut oil

MEYER LEMON COCONUT BUTTER

Yields ½ cup

¼ cup O meyer lemon extra virgin olive oil

¼ cup melted virgin coconut oil

ROASTED GARLIC COCONUT BUTTER

Yields ½ cup

¼ cup O roasted garlic extra virgin olive oil

¼ cup melted virgin coconut oil

For all recipes, blend together olive oil and melted coconut oil in small glass jar with a lid until well mixed. Place lid on jar and store in refrigerator until solid. Use as a butter substitute.

*Raw Vegan

3-HERB PESTO

Makes around 1½ cups

THIS 3-HERB PESTO is a nut-free, cheese-free pesto that is fresh, herbaceous, and full of bright citrus flavor. Basil, parsley, and cilantro are 3 of my favorite health-promoting herbs. Include them in your diet on a weekly basis and enjoy all the health benefits they provide. Try this pesto on your favorite fish, tossed with buckwheat, quinoa, or brown rice pasta, mixed in goat cheese, on scrambled eggs, or tossed with your favorite raw or steamed vegetables or salad greens.

3 cups loosely packed fresh basil leaves—rinsed and patted dry

½ cup flat-leaf parsley leaves—rinsed and patted dry

½ cup cilantro leaves—rinsed and patted dry

2 cloves peeled garlic—grated on a Microplane

1 teaspoon unrefined sea salt

¼ teaspoon fresh ground black pepper

1 tablespoon fresh lemon juice

¼ teaspoon lemon zest

⅓–½ cup extra virgin olive oil

Place basil, parsley, cilantro, garlic, sea salt, black pepper, lemon juice, and lemon zest in a food processor. Process all ingredients until finely chopped, scraping down sides of bowl. With machine running, add the olive oil in a thin stream until pesto has thickened. Taste and add more sea salt or olive oil if needed. Transfer pesto to covered container and pour small amount of olive oil on top of surface. Cover and refrigerate for up to 2 weeks or freeze for up to 3 months. ✎

ARUGULA SPINACH WALNUT PESTO

Follow above recipe, substituting 2 cups of baby or wild arugula and 2 cups baby spinach for the herbs. Add ¼ cup finely chopped raw walnuts. Substitute cold pressed walnut oil for the olive oil and fresh orange juice and orange zest for the lemon juice and zest. ✎ *Raw Vegan

FRESH AND CULTURED MAYONNAISE

Makes around 1½ cups

2 large egg yolks at room temperature

1 teaspoon Dijon mustard

2 teaspoons fresh lemon juice

2 teaspoons raw apple cider vinegar

1 teaspoon unrefined sea salt

½ cup extra virgin olive oil

½ cup walnut or avocado oil

1 tablespoon liquid whey—optional (recipe on page 64)

Place small mixing bowl on top of folded towel. Place egg yolks, mustard, lemon juice, apple cider vinegar, and sea salt in bowl and whisk with wire whisk until well blended, for around 60 seconds. Slowly add the oil into the egg mixture while whisking vigorously and blend until creamy and thick. Taste and adjust seasoning. If mayonnaise breaks, add another room-temperature egg yolk and continue blending until mayonnaise comes together. If you want cultured mayonnaise, stir in whey, cover mayonnaise, and let sit at room temperature for 6–7 hours before refrigerating. If no whey is added, refrigerate in a glass container with lid immediately. Mayonnaise lasts 1 week without whey or 1 month with whey. ↝

WHITE BALSAMIC MAYONNAISE

Follow recipe for mayonnaise using white balsamic vinegar for apple cider vinegar. ↝

HONEY DIJON MAYONNAISE

Follow recipe for mayonnaise but reduce salt to ¼ teaspoon and blend 2 tablespoons Dijon mustard into mayonnaise in place of the 1 teaspoon of mustard. When mayonnaise is thick, slowly stir in 1 tablespoon of raw honey. ↝

THAI BASIL LIME MAYONNAISE

Thai purple sweet basil has purple stems and a mild licorice flavor that is great with mayonnaise. Follow the basic recipe; substitute lime juice for the lemon, and stir in 2 tablespoons minced fresh Thai basil into 1 cup of finished mayonnaise. ↝

YOGURT GOAT CHEESE AND WHEY

Makes around 3 cups cream cheese and 1 cup whey

HOMEMADE GOAT CHEESE tastes creamy, rich, tangy, and delicious with healthy enzymes and probiotics to boost digestion. Try this probiotic-rich version made with goat's milk yogurt and taste the difference. I like the Redwood Hill Farm brand of goat yogurt. The liquid probiotic-rich whey which drains from the yogurt is perfect for using to make my cultured vegetables, cultured apple goji berry compote, cultured salsa, and mayonnaise. You can also use plain organic whole milk or raw cow's milk yogurt with active cultures if you can't find or don't like goat yogurt.

1 (32-ounce) container goat's milk yogurt or plain organic whole cow's milk yogurt

Place a mesh strainer inside a larger bowl. Line the strainer with a thin, clean dish towel or tripled pieces of cheesecloth. Pour the yogurt in the towel or cheesecloth, cover, and let the yogurt sit in the refrigerator overnight until the whey drips into the bowl and the yogurt gets thick. Pour whey into glass jar with lid. Remove yogurt cheese from towel or cloth and place in a clean glass jar with a lid. Place goat cheese and whey in the refrigerator and use in a variety of different recipes. Yogurt cheese lasts for 3–4 weeks in the refrigerator, and whey lasts for up to 6 weeks. ↪

TOMATO TARRAGON GOAT CHEESE

¾ cup yogurt goat cheese

3 tablespoons chopped oven-dried tomatoes (recipe on page 60)

1 tablespoon fresh minced tarragon leaves

1 teaspoon fresh lemon juice

LEMON DILL GOAT CHEESE

¾ cup yogurt goat cheese

2 tablespoons fresh minced dill leaves

1 tablespoon fresh lemon juice

1 teaspoon lemon zest

For both recipe variations, mix all ingredients together in a small bowl until well blended. Will last covered in the refrigerator for 1–2 weeks. Serve goat cheese on lettuce leaves, cucumber slices, celery sticks, or on sprouted or fermented whole grain toast. ↪

CULTURED TOMATO PINEAPPLE SALSA

Makes around 5 cups

MY HOMEMADE CULTURED SALSA is a probiotic-rich salsa that contains juicy tomatoes, sweet, enzyme-rich pineapple, and fragrant cilantro that is totally refreshing and delicious. These ingredients are full of health-promoting nutrients like lycopene, vitamin C, beta-carotene, and fiber. Enjoy this enzyme-packed salsa with guacamole, fresh vegetables, or on baked or grilled fish. Leave seeds and membranes in jalapeño chili pepper if you like your salsa spicy.

4 cups roma tomatoes—skin removed and rough chopped

1 small red onion—peeled and rough chopped

2 small cloves peeled garlic

1 cup cubed pineapple

1 jalapeño chili pepper—seeds and membranes removed

2 tablespoons fresh lime juice

2 teaspoons unrefined sea salt

⅓ cup organic cilantro leaves

1 packet vegetable culture starter or ⅓ cup liquid whey (recipe on page 64)

1 Clean 1½-quart large mouth glass jar with lid

In a food processor, pulse all the salsa ingredients except cilantro and culture starter or whey until it has the consistency of a smooth blended salsa. If using culture starter, mix starter with ¼ cup of 90° F warm filtered water with ½ teaspoon of coconut sugar or Sucanat added and let mixture sit for 20 minutes to allow the good bacteria to wake up. Pour salsa into a bowl and stir in cilantro leaves and whey or culture starter mixture. Place salsa into the clean, dry jar and leave at least 2 inches of space at top of the jar. Cover jar with lid and ferment salsa at room temperature away from light for 2 days. After culturing salsa, refrigerate covered for up to 6 to 8 weeks. Each time you serve this salsa, use a spoon to push remaining salsa under the liquid so it stays fresh. ✎

*Raw Vegan

CULTURED APPLE GOJI BERRY COMPOTE

Makes around 5 cups

THIS CULTURED APPLE GOJI BERRY COMPOTE is a great way to enjoy the benefits of cultured foods if you are new to them. Both adults and children will enjoy this sweet compote with delicious spices that add warmth to the body. Enjoy this compote on its own or with other foods and reap the benefits of all the healing probiotics and enzymes! If you don't have goji berries, you can substitute other unsulfured dried fruits like currants, raisins, cherries, or cranberries.

5 medium organic Fuji apples—cored, unpeeled, and cut in half

1 peeled orange

½ teaspoon unrefined sea salt

3 tablespoons coconut sugar, Rapadura, or Sucanat

2 teaspoons organic cinnamon

1 teaspoon fresh peeled ginger—grated

1 cup filtered or spring water (warm to 90° F)

1 package vegetable culture starter or ⅓ cup liquid whey (recipe on page 64)

⅓ cup goji berries

1 Clean 1½-quart large mouth glass jar with lid

Place 1 cored apple, the peeled orange, sea salt, sweetener of choice, cinnamon, ginger, and water in blender and blend until juice mixture is smooth, around 60 seconds. In a large bowl, stir apple juice mixture and culture starter together and let sit at room temperature for 20 minutes to allow good bacteria to start feeding on the sugars in the apple mixture. If using whey, you can skip this step and just stir whey into juice mixture. Place remaining 4 apples in food processor and pulse until finely chopped. Mix the chopped apples together with the apple juice mixture and goji berries in a large bowl and stir until well combined and the fruits are completely coated with the liquid. Spoon the apple goji berry compote in the clean glass jar and mash down so that the apples release their juice and are completely covered with the liquid. Leave at least 2 inches of space at the top of the jar to allow compote to expand. Place lid on jar and ferment compote at room temperature away from light for 2 days. After culturing compote, place in refrigerator for up to 2 months. ↩

*Raw Vegan

DREAMY DRINKS

DREAMY DRINKS ARE QUICK LIQUID NUTRITION THAT IS PERFECT FOR BUSY PEOPLE ON THE GO WHO WANT TO MAKE HEALTHY BEVERAGE CHOICES THAT ARE EASY TO DIGEST AND CAN PROVIDE ENERGY AND HEALING. USE THESE BEVERAGES TO REPLACE SOFT DRINKS, BOTTLED JUICES, AND SPORTS DRINKS THAT USE HIGH FRUCTOSE CORN SYRUP, ARTIFICIAL SWEETENERS, AND OTHER INGREDIENTS THAT ARE HEALTH DEPLETING.

THESE DREAMY DRINKS TASTE DIVINE AND ARE A SIMPLE WAY TO GET TONS OF NUTRIENTS THAT YOUR BODY WILL LOVE. THE DREAMY DRINKS IN THIS SECTION INCLUDE CREAMY NUT AND SEED MILKS, GREEN ENERGY SMOOTHIES, ELIXIRS, TONICS, AND FERMENTED OR CULTURED DRINKS.

I HAVE GIVEN RECIPES FOR MY FAVORITE DRINKS, BUT FEEL FREE TO USE THEM AS A GUIDELINE TO CREATE YOUR OWN COMBINATIONS OF DRINKS BASED ON INGREDIENTS THAT YOU HAVE ON HAND OR CAN PURCHASE AT YOUR LOCAL MARKET. YOU CAN SUBSTITUTE FILTERED OR SPRING WATER FOR THE LIQUIDS IN THE GREEN ENERGY SMOOTHIES, BUT YOU WON'T GET THE ADDITIONAL AMOUNT OF NUTRIENTS THAT THE NUT OR SEED MILKS AND COCONUT WATER PROVIDES.

I HAVE GIVEN SOME CHOICES OF NATURAL SWEETENERS TO USE IN MY RECIPES FROM THE LIST OF CHOICES THAT I MENTIONED EARLIER IN THIS BOOK. USE THESE CHOICES AS A GUIDELINE AND FEEL FREE TO SUBSTITUTE THE SWEETENER WHICH YOU PREFER DEPENDING ON YOUR HEALTH NEEDS AND TASTES.

I HAVE NOTED THE RECIPES THAT ARE VEGAN. SOME OF THESE RECIPES USE RAW HONEY, WHICH IS NOT VEGAN. HOWEVER, MANY VEGANS USE RAW HONEY EVEN THOUGH IT COMES FROM BEES BECAUSE OF THE TASTE AND NUTRITIONAL BENEFITS ASSOCIATED WITH RAW HONEY. YOU CAN SUBSTITUTE DRIED FRUIT, STEVIA, MAPLE SYRUP, COCONUT SUGAR, COCONUT NECTAR, OR YACON IF YOU ARE A VEGAN WHO ONLY WANTS TO USE A VEGAN SWEETENER.

■ CREAMY NUT AND SEED MILKS

This section includes recipes for nut and seed milks that are a creamy, yummy substitute for dairy. Many people cannot digest pasteurized dairy because the enzymes and beneficial bacteria which allow you to digest the lactose or milk sugar and casein or milk protein have been destroyed during the high heat pasteurization of the dairy. If you drink cow's milk, organic cultured or raw dairy from grass-fed cows is the best choice because cultured or raw dairy retains the enzymes and beneficial lactobacillus bacteria, which help you, digest the lactose and casein.

Cultured or fermented dairy has lactic acid, which increases the absorption of key minerals in the dairy. For people who can't or prefer not to drink dairy, nut and seed milks make a good option, because when made by you, they are not heat-pasteurized, are free of hormones, antibiotics, and steroids that are present in factory-farm, nonorganic, heat-pasteurized dairy products. Nut or seed milks are very versatile and can be consumed as is, used in your smoothies, and used in most recipes that use milk. I've created all of the nut and seed milk recipes in this cookbook with raw nuts or seeds that don't have enzyme inhibitors, or with nuts or seeds or nut or seed butters that are sprouted and don't need soaking just in case you are too busy or don't want to soak your nuts or seeds. For sprouted nuts and seeds, I recommend using the Better than Roasted by Blue Mountain Organics, Go Raw, Gone Nuts, Living Nutz, or Wilderness Family Naturals nuts and seeds or nut and seed butters because these companies soak their organic raw nuts and seeds, sprout them, and dehydrate them at low temperatures, which removes their enzyme inhibitors and increases their digestibility.

If you want to only use raw nut or seed butters, realize they will have enzyme inhibitors and may be difficult to digest for some people. Taking a plant-based enzyme supplement with raw nuts or seeds can aid your digestion of them. If you do decide to soak your own nuts and seeds before using, I have included guidelines to show you how to soak them. For all my nut or seed milk recipes which use nut or seed butters, substitute 1¼ cups of soaked raw nuts or seeds for the nut or seed butters used in the recipe and use the 3 cups of water listed in the recipe.

RECIPE AND GUIDELINES FOR SOAKING NUTS AND SEEDS

MOST RAW NUTS AND SEEDS HAVE ANTI-NUTRIENTS that protect them from sprouting or germinating until the right conditions are met. When you soak nuts or seeds in salted water, it will release the enzyme inhibitors, activate the enzymes, and increase key vitamins. Soaking allows nuts and seeds to start the process of germination. Sprouting turns them into living food and increases the nutrient content.

4 cups raw nuts or seeds of your choice

1 tablespoon unrefined sea salt

5 cups filtered or spring water

Place nuts or seeds in a bowl with water and sea salt. Stir, cover with thin towel, and leave on the counter top for the recommended times. After soaking is done, drain off the soaking water, rinse with fresh water, and drain again. Use soaked nuts or seeds to make milk, or store nuts or seeds in the refrigerator covered for 2 days. To make milk, add 1¼ cups of soaked nuts/seeds in blender with 3 cups of filtered or spring water and blend until smooth. Once you make the milk with these soaked nuts or seeds, you can strain it with a nut bag or fine mesh strainer for a smoother consistency. All of the prepared unsweetened nut and seed milks will last for 3–5 days in the refrigerator or can be frozen. Create my fruit-based milk recipes using the plain nut or seed milks for the water and nut or seed butters listed in the recipe. Another option is to place soaked nuts or seeds in an oven set at 150° F or in a dehydrator set at 115° F and bake until the nuts or seeds are dry and crisp. This can take from 10–24 hours, depending on whether you choose to use an oven or a dehydrator. Baking nuts and seeds at a low temperature protects the important fats from oxidation and preserves the enzymes. Some nuts and seeds are low in anti-nutrients and don't need soaking before eating. These include: Macadamia nuts, brazil nuts, and hemp seeds. If using these nuts or seeds with low anti-nutrients in recipes that require them to be soft, only soak for 1–2 hours. Most raw cashews have been heated to remove the inner and outer shells and aren't really raw. When chia seeds are soaked, don't use salt in the water or drain the water. Chia seeds create an edible gel and don't need to be rinsed. ✎

SUGGESTED SOAKING TIMES

Hard nuts or seeds: soak overnight or up to 8–10 hours.

These include almonds, chia seeds, hazelnuts, and buckwheat groats.

Soft nuts or seeds: soak for 4–6 hours.

These include pecans, walnuts, pumpkin seeds, sesame seeds, sunflower seeds, and pistachios.

Nuts and Seeds that only need 1–2 hours.

These include pine nuts, flax seeds, and cashews. ✎

CARROT PECAN MILK

Yields around 4½ cups

CARROTS are chock full of beta-carotene and fiber. Blending the carrots in a high-powered blender helps break down the cell walls and makes the carrots' nutrients more available for your body to easily absorb. Pecans have B vitamins, vitamin E, iron, magnesium, manganese, copper, molybdenum, and potassium. Pecans also have a large amount of plant sterols which are good for helping to lower our cholesterol levels naturally. Combining the sweet carrots with buttery pecans provides your body with healthy fats and key nutrients that will make you feel energized and strong. The light orange color of this milk and delicious taste will put a smile on your face!

3 cups filtered or spring water

4 tablespoons sprouted or raw pecan butter or 1¼ cups soaked raw pecans

2 medium organic carrots—tops removed, peeled, and chopped

1½ teaspoons cinnamon

1 crushed cardamom pod or ¼ teaspoon cardamom powder

2 teaspoons pure vanilla extract

2 tablespoons organic maple syrup, 2 pitted soft dates, or stevia to taste

Blend all ingredients in a blender until smooth and creamy. Taste and make sweeter if you like. Strain milk through nut milk bag or fine mesh strainer to remove any pulp. Drink as is or use to blend into smoothies. Milk will last for 2–3 days covered in the refrigerator.

*Raw Vegan

ORANGE GINGER PUMPKIN SEED MILK

Yields around 4½ cups

PUMPKIN SEEDS OR PEPITAS MAKE SWEET, creamy milk that contains vitamin A, B vitamins, iron, zinc, magnesium, and manganese. Pumpkin seeds are also a good source of protein and monounsaturated fats.

3 cups filtered or spring water
4 tablespoons sprouted or raw pumpkin seed butter or 1¼ cups soaked pumpkin seeds
3 tablespoons coconut sugar, 3 pitted soft dates, or stevia to taste
1 teaspoon fresh peeled ginger—grated
¼ cup fresh orange juice
¼ teaspoon grated orange zest

Blend all ingredients in a blender until creamy and smooth. Taste and add more sweetener if you like sweeter pumpkin seed milk. Strain with a nut bag or fine mesh strainer if using the pumpkin seeds. Drink as is or use to blend into smoothies. Milk will last for 3–5 days in the refrigerator. ✑

*Raw Vegan

VANILLA BRAZIL NUT MILK

Yields around 4½ cups

Brazil nuts create a delectable, creamy nut milk that is high in the mineral selenium. I love to make this recipe with vanilla beans because the vanilla flavor is more intense.

3 cups filtered or spring water
1¼ cups raw Brazil nuts—soaked 1 hour and drained
3 tablespoons coconut sugar, 3 pitted soft dates, or stevia to taste
1 teaspoon cinnamon
Seeds from 1 vanilla bean or 1 tablespoon pure vanilla extract

Blend all ingredients in a blender until creamy and smooth. Taste and add more sweetener if you like sweeter nut milk. Strain with a nut bag or fine mesh strainer. Drink as is or use to blend into smoothies. Milk will last for 3–5 days covered in the refrigerator. ✑

*Raw Vegan

MANGO CASHEW MILK

Yields around 4½ cups

MANGOS are one of the most popular fruits in the world due to their lush texture and amazing, sweet flavor. Mangos are full of fiber, vitamin A, vitamin C, vitamin E, B vitamins, carotenes, copper, and magnesium, which provide your body with plenty of important nutrients. Mangos are also around 82 percent water, which helps to hydrate your body. The mango and cashew create delectable, creamy milk that you can enjoy in a variety of different recipes.

3 cups filtered or spring water

4 tablespoons raw cashew butter or 1¼ cups soaked raw cashews

1½ cups mango chunks

2 tablespoons coconut sugar, 2 pitted soft dates, or stevia to taste

Blend all ingredients in a blender until creamy and smooth. Taste and make sweeter if you like. Strain with a nut bag or fine mesh strainer if using the cashews. Drink as is or use to blend into smoothies. Milk will last for 2–3 days covered in the refrigerator.

*Raw Vegan

NECTARINE WALNUT MILK

Yields around 4½ cups

NECTARINES are one of my favorite fruits, especially when in season in the summer when they are extra juicy and sweet. Nectarines provide your body with flavonoids, carotenes, lycopene, potassium, and fiber. Nectarines are a stone fruit with a beautiful yellow flesh which continues to ripen even after it is picked from the tree. Nectarines name comes from the Greek word "nektar" which means sweet liquid. Conventionally raised nectarines are heavily sprayed with pesticides, so always purchase organic.

3 cups filtered or spring water

4 tablespoons sprouted or raw walnut butter or 1¼ cups soaked walnuts

2 organic nectarines—cut in half, remove pits

2 teaspoons pure vanilla extract

¼ teaspoon cinnamon

1 tablespoon raw honey, 2 pitted soft dates, or stevia to taste

Blend all ingredients in a blender until creamy and smooth. Taste and make sweeter if you like. Strain with a nut bag or fine mesh strainer if using the walnuts. Drink as is or use to blend into smoothies. Milk will last for 3–4 days covered in the refrigerator.

*Raw Vegan

BANANA HEMP SEED MILK

Yields around 4½ cups

HEMP SEEDS are an amazing superfood that is both appetizing and nutrient-rich. The pretty light green color and crunchy texture is fantastic. Hemp seeds have all the essential amino acids and are full of fiber. Hemp seeds are also a good source of protein and have the perfect balance of essential fatty acids omega-3 and 6. Vanilla adds a wonderful, warm taste that blends well with the nutty flavor of the hemp seeds. Bananas are a delicious, creamy fruit that is full of potassium, vitamin C and vitamin B6. Bananas are also a good source of soluble fiber that will help keep your digestive system healthy. Try to purchase only fair trade or organic bananas. When bananas are combined with the hemp seeds, you get a superfood powerhouse.

3 cups filtered or spring water

1 cup hemp seeds (unsoaked)

2 teaspoons pure vanilla extract

2 peeled bananas—organic or fair trade

2 tablespoons coconut sugar, 2 pitted soft dates, or stevia to taste

¼ teaspoon cinnamon

Blend all ingredients in a blender until creamy and smooth. Taste and make sweeter if you like. Drink as is or use to blend into smoothies. Milk will last for 2–3 days covered in the refrigerator. ⤳

*Raw Vegan

CAROB ALMOND MILK

Yields around 4½ cups

CAROB is a fruit pod from a tropical tree in the legume family. Carob is high in protein, calcium, vitamin A, B vitamins, potassium, and fiber. Carob is caffeine-free and low in fat with a taste very similar to chocolate with caramel overtones. Carob contains water-soluble tannins which help bind up toxins in your gastrointestinal (GI) tract so they can be removed safely from your body.

3 cups filtered or spring water

4 tablespoons sprouted or raw almond butter or 1¼ cups soaked almonds

¼ cup carob powder

1 tablespoon organic maple syrup, 2 pitted soft dates, or stevia to taste

¼ teaspoon cinnamon

1 teaspoon pure vanilla extract

Blend all ingredients in a blender until creamy and smooth. Taste and make sweeter if you like. Strain with a nut bag or fine mesh strainer if using the almonds. Drink as is or use to blend into smoothies. Milk will last for 3–5 days covered in the refrigerator. ✎

*Raw Vegan

VANILLA PISTACHIO MILK

Yields around 4½ cups

THIS PISTACHIO MILK is one of my favorite milks because it tastes delicious, has a cool light green color, and is very creamy and filling. Pistachios are an ancient nut that contains protein, copper, zinc, B vitamins, vitamin E, folic acid, magnesium, potassium, and fiber. Pistachios' fat content is primarily heart-healthy monounsaturated fat.

3 cups filtered or spring water

4 tablespoons sprouted or raw pistachio nut butter or 1¼ cups soaked raw pistachio nuts

3 tablespoons coconut sugar, 3 pitted soft dates, or stevia to taste

1 tablespoon pure vanilla extract or seeds from 1 vanilla bean

Blend all ingredients in a blender until creamy and smooth. Taste and make sweeter if you like. Strain with a nut bag or fine mesh strainer if using pistachio nuts. Drink as is or use to blend in smoothies. Milk will last for 3–5 days covered in refrigerator. ✎

*Raw Vegan

COCONUT MILK 2 WAYS

THESE QUICK MILKS are a great solution for making a quick batch of fresh coconut milk that is nutrient-rich, preservative free, and delicious. The young coconuts you need for this recipe have an outer white shell and pointed end. Mature coconuts have a brown outer shell. If you are unsure of how to open these coconuts or hesitant about doing it yourself, then feel free to ask the store where you purchase them to crack them open for you and give you the coconut water inside. Once you get home, you can scrape the inside of the coconut with the back of a large spoon or small spatula to remove the meat. The second recipe uses packaged coconut water and unsweetened dried coconut if you don't have access to young coconuts. I love coconuts because they taste yummy and have wonderful health-promoting properties. Coconuts are a good source of antioxidants and minerals. Coconuts contain high amounts of lauric acid and capric acid, which are fatty acids that have antibacterial, anti-viral, and anti-microbial properties. These medium chain fatty acids are used for energy production and are easier for your body to digest.

FRESH COCONUT MILK

Yields around 4 cups

3½ cups young coconut water
2 cups young coconut meat
Small pinch unrefined sea salt

Place coconut water, coconut meat, and sea salt in the blender and blend until smooth and creamy. Enjoy immediately in any recipes that call for coconut milk, or if you can't find canned coconut milk that has no preservatives. This coconut milk will last for 3–5 days covered in the refrigerator or can be frozen for up to 1 month for later use. ৲

COCONUT MILK USING DRIED COCONUT

Yields around 4½ cups

2 cups unsweetened dried coconut flakes
4 cups young coconut water
Small pinch unrefined sea salt

Soak dried coconut flakes in coconut water for 30–40 minutes until soft. Place in a blender and blend until smooth. Strain out any remaining coconut flakes with a nut bag or mesh strainer. Use this milk in any recipes that call for coconut milk. This coconut milk will last for 5–7 days covered in the refrigerator or can be frozen for up to 1 month for later use. ৲

*Raw Vegan

■ GREEN ENERGY SMOOTHIES

GREEN ENERGY SMOOTHIES are one of my favorite drinks! Green energy smoothies are a great way to pack a lot of whole food nutrients into a sweet, fruity, alkalizing drink that's easy to make and digest. Green energy smoothies are extremely satisfying, health promoting, great for travel, and the perfect choice for helping you stay energized and focused without feeling weighed down or sluggish.

Drinking green energy smoothies on a regular basis will:

- Increase alkalinity in your body while reducing acid buildup.
- Help strengthen your immune system.
- Allow you to safely clean and detoxify your body.
- Help you lose weight in an easy and effective way.
- Substantially increase your energy level and stamina.
- Promote better digestion and assimilation of key nutrients.

Feel free to add between 2 to 4 cups of leafy greens depending on your taste. I love 3 or 4 cups of greens in my personal smoothies. This addition will help you get a good amount of green leafy vegetables into your diet on a regular basis, which will make a big difference in your well-being. Make sure you rotate your greens during the week so that you can take advantage of the wide variety of nutrients each green provides. Have fun experimenting and see what combinations work for you. I also like to include more protein and nutrients with raw organic protein powder by Boku, Garden of Life, or Vega, hemp protein powder by Nutiva, Living Harvest, or Manitoba Harvest, or greens and fruit superfoods like Vitamineral Green by HealthForce Nutritionals, Raw Reserve by Amazing Grass, or VitaForce. Another great nutrient booster is adding your favorite individual superfoods like spirulina or maca by E3 Live, Vivapura, HealthForce Nutritionals, Essential Living Foods, Amazing Grass, Garden of Life, Navitas Naturals, or Ultimate Superfoods. You can buy these products at your local health food store or from each company's Web site.

All of my green energy smoothies use nut or seed milks or coconut water and coconut milk as the liquid base. I also like to use homemade ice cubes out of nut or seed milk, coconut water, coconut kefir, raw milk, milk kefir, or fresh vegetable juices when I use fresh fruit to make cold, creamy smoothies without diluting the flavor by using water-based ice cubes. Doing this also adds additional nutrients. You can also use frozen fruit to re-create the same cold, creamy texture.

BING CHERRY SMOOTHIE

Serves 2

CALIFORNIA ALMONDS HAVE A SMOOTH, buttery taste that blends wonderfully with the cherries. Almonds are a rich source of flavonoids, protein, vitamin E, potassium, calcium, iron, magnesium, and fiber. Sweet Bing cherries have a beautiful, dark red, almost violet color and plump, juicy texture that is wonderful in this smoothie. Cherries are a good source of vitamin C, melatonin, and copper. Cherries also contain a high amount of flavonoids, which reduce inflammation in the body and help lower uric acid levels.

3 cups carob almond milk (recipe on page 78)

2 cups fresh or frozen pitted organic Bing cherries

2–3 cups organic lolla rossa or red oak leaf lettuce

¼ teaspoon cinnamon

Your favorite protein powder or superfood—optional

Blend all ingredients in a blender until smooth and creamy. Taste and add a natural sweetener of choice if needed. Serve immediately. ⌒

*Raw Vegan

WILD BLUEBERRY SMOOTHIE

Serves 2

WILD BLUEBERRIES are an amazing superfood fruit that is easy to find at your local farmers' markets or favorite food store. Their dark blue color and sweet flavor make a wonderful smoothie and will provide your body with key vitamins, minerals, fiber, and phytonutrients. This smoothie is a great introduction into drinking green smoothies, especially if you are apprehensive about the green color, because the blueberries make the smoothie purple instead of green and the spinach is a mild leafy green so you can't taste it in the smoothie.

3 cups vanilla Brazil nut milk (recipe on page 74)

2 cups fresh or frozen wild or organic blueberries

1 peeled banana—organic or fair trade

2–3 cups organic baby spinach

1 small avocado—peeled and pitted

¼ teaspoon cinnamon

Your favorite protein powder or superfood—optional

Place all ingredients in a blender and blend until smooth and creamy. Taste and add a natural sweetener of choice if needed. Serve immediately. ᴄᴀ

*Raw Vegan

PEACH CUCUMBER SMOOTHIE

Serves 2

THIS UNIQUE SMOOTHIE contains Persian cucumbers, which are a sweet cucumber with a thin outer skin that is a wonderful source of silica, vitamin C, vitamin A, and fiber. The coconut water is an isotonic beverage which contains electrolytes which hydrate and keep your body balanced. The sweet peaches add key antioxidants and additional nutrients to the mix. Seek out freestone peaches, which are the best peaches for enjoying raw.

3 cups young coconut water

2 cups fresh organic freestone peaches—pitted and rough chopped

2 organic Persian cucumbers—rough chopped

2–3 cups organic green oak leaf lettuce

½ cup organic unsweetened coconut milk—preservative free

Blend all ingredients in a blender until smooth and creamy. Taste and add a natural sweetener of choice if needed. Serve immediately. ᴖ

STRAWBERRY BANANA MACA SMOOTHIE

Serves 2

MACA ROOT is an amazing adaptogen root vegetable from the Andes Mountains in Peru. It is reported to increase energy, libido, strength, and athletic performance. Maca is mineral-rich and has twenty amino acids, including essential amino acids. Maca is also considered useful for balancing hormones and rebuilding our adrenal glands, which is great for anyone who has a lot of stress in his or her life. Blending maca with potassium-rich banana hemp milk, and juicy strawberries gives your body that extra boost of good nutrition to start your day off right.

3 cups banana hemp seed milk (recipe on page 77)

2 cups fresh or frozen organic strawberries

2–3 cups organic romaine lettuce

2 teaspoons maca root powder

1 teaspoon pure vanilla extract

Blend all ingredients in a blender until smooth and creamy. Taste and add a natural sweetener of choice if needed. Serve immediately. ᴖ

*Raw Vegan

PAPAYA SMOOTHIE

Serves 2

PAPAYAS have a bright orange, juicy flesh and black seeds that can be dried, ground up, and used like black pepper. Papayas are filled with powerful antioxidants, potassium, calcium, flavonoids, and fiber. Papayas also contain papain, which is a great digestive enzyme for protein. Papayas combined with the vanilla Brazil nut milk and butter lettuce will provide you with chlorophyll, phytonutrients, and healthy fat, which can help increase your digestive power and strengthen your immune system. I like to use spirulina crunchies in this smoothie. Spirulina crunchies are a blue green micro algae that gives an added punch of protein, antioxidants, iron, and calcium, but the smoothie is also good without them. Green Tara and Vivapura both sell spirulina crunchies.

3 cups vanilla Brazil nut milk (recipe on page 74)

2 cups fresh or frozen papaya chunks

2–3 cups organic butter lettuce

1 teaspoon fresh lemon juice

2 tablespoons spirulina crunchies—optional

Blend all ingredients with 1 tablespoon of spirulina crunchies in a blender until smooth and creamy. Taste and add a natural sweetener of choice if needed. Top with additional spirulina if using. Serve immediately. ᓭ

*Raw Vegan

DELICIOUSLY HOLISTIC

CHOCOLATE RASPBERRY SMOOTHIE

Serves 2

THIS RICH CHOCOLATE FRUIT SMOOTHIE has a high level of nutrients that come from the raw cacao, raspberries, carob almond milk, and green oak leaf lettuce. Luscious raspberries are filled with calcium, B vitamins, vitamin C, potassium, magnesium, flavonoids, and fiber. Green leaf lettuce contains chlorophyll, vitamin C, B vitamins, and chromium. The raw cacao powder adds large amounts of flavonoids, protein, and magnesium. Cacao does have caffeine which can stimulate you, so if you are sensitive to this, please feel free to substitute carob powder.

3 cups carob almond milk (recipe on page 78)

2 cups fresh or frozen raspberries

2 tablespoons raw cacao powder

1 peeled banana—organic or fair trade

2–3 cups organic green oak leaf lettuce

1 teaspoon pure vanilla extract

2 tablespoons coconut sugar or stevia to taste

Your favorite protein powder or superfood—optional

⅛ cup raw cacao nibs—optional

Blend all ingredients except cacao nibs in a blender until smooth and creamy. Pour into glasses and top with raw cacao nibs if using. Serve immediately. ⌒

*Raw Vegan

MANGO RASBERRY SPIRULINA SMOOTHIE

Serves 2

SUCCULENT MANGOS are one of my absolute favorite health-promoting fruits. Mangos are revered around the world for their wonderful taste and healing properties. Mangos are a potent cancer fighter due to their high levels of antioxidants, carotenoids, phytochemicals, iron, vitamin A, and enzymes. When you add in the nutrient-rich sweet and tart raspberries you get a smoothie that is both delicious and healing to the body. I like to use spirulina crunchies in this smoothie. Green Tara and Vivapura both sell spirulina crunchies. Spirulina crunchies are blue green micro algae that give an added punch of protein, antioxidants, iron, and calcium, but the smoothie is also good without them. Feel free to try both ways and see which one you prefer.

3 cups mango cashew milk (recipe on page 75)

2 cups fresh or frozen raspberries

2–3 cups organic romaine lettuce

2 tablespoons spirulina crunchies—optional

Blend all ingredients with 1 tablespoon of spirulina crunchies in a blender until smooth and creamy. Taste and add a natural sweetener of choice if needed. Top with additional spirulina and raspberries and serve immediately. ᑌ

*Raw Vegan

ACAI BERRY CRANBERRY SMOOTHIE

Serves 2

ACAI BERRIES, also known as Brazilian palm berries, have a flavor that is a cross between a berry and chocolate. These superfood berries are packed full of antioxidants, vitamins, and minerals that will nourish and provide your body with top quality nutrition. Kale has a mild flavor which works well in this smoothie. Kale is one of my favorite leafy greens, and it is filled with phytonutrients and anti-cancer compounds which help strengthen your immune system.

3 cups vanilla pistachio milk (recipe on page 78)

1 packet Sambazon Acai berry puree

2 cups fresh or frozen cranberries

2–3 cups organic Kale—around 4 or 5 leaves (remove stems)

1 teaspoon pure vanilla extract

¼ teaspoon cinnamon

2 tablespoons coconut sugar, or ¼ teaspoon or 2 packets stevia

Your favorite protein powder or superfood—optional

Place all ingredients in a blender and blend until smooth and creamy. Taste and add more natural sweetener if needed. Serve immediately. ⌒

*Raw Vegan

CHERRY GOJI BERRY SMOOTHIE

Serves 2

THIS FANTASTIC SMOOTHIE features 3 nutritional powerhouses: kale, goji berries, and cherries. Kale is a member of the cruciferous family and is one of the most nutrient-dense leafy greens on the planet, with high levels of protein, vitamin A, vitamin C, iron, potassium, calcium, folic acid, and phytonutrients. Chinese Goji berries contain 18 amino acids, including eight essential amino acids, beta-carotene, B vitamins, and vitamin C. One ounce of goji berries has 4 grams of protein. Cherries help fight inflammation and contain flavonoids and copper. The Goji berries add additional nutrients to your smoothie recipe, but if you can't purchase them you can make the recipe without them.

3 cups orange ginger pumpkin seed milk (recipe on page 74)

2 cups fresh or frozen pitted organic cherries

2–3 cups organic dinosaur kale—around 4 or 5 leaves (remove stems)

¼ cup goji berries—soaked in orange ginger pumpkin seed milk for 20 minutes

Your favorite protein powder or superfood—optional

Blend all ingredients in a blender until smooth and creamy. Taste and add a natural sweetener of choice if needed. Serve immediately. ✎

*Raw Vegan

BLUEBERRY POMEGRANATE SMOOTHIE

Serves 2

BLUEBERRIES are "super berries" because blueberries are full of fiber, polyphenols, antioxidants, vitamin C, vitamin E, carotenoids, iron, potassium, and magnesium. Blueberries also contain over 25 phytochemicals, which protect the body from free radicals. By combining blueberries with nutrient-rich spinach and the powerful pomegranate, you get a smoothie that can help protect you against a wide range of degenerative diseases.

3 cups vanilla Brazil nut milk (recipe on page 74)

1 cup pomegranate seeds

2 cups fresh or frozen wild or organic blueberries

2–3 cups organic baby spinach

¼ teaspoon cinnamon

Your favorite protein powder or superfood—optional

Place all ingredients in a blender and blend until smooth and creamy. Taste and add a natural sweetener of choice if needed. Serve immediately. ↩

*Raw Vegan

NECTARINE SMOOTHIE

Serves 2

JUICY NECTARINES are one of my favorite stone fruits. They are full of flavonoids, vitamins, minerals, and fiber which help protect the body against cancer, heart disease, and inflammation. When combined with the nectarine walnut milk you have a potent, delicious, nutrient-filled smoothie that is also extremely hydrating.

3 cups nectarine walnut milk (recipe on page 75)

2 cups fresh or frozen organic nectarines—pitted and rough chopped

2–3 cups organic red oak leaf lettuce

1 teaspoon pure vanilla extract

¼ teaspoon cinnamon

Your favorite protein powder or superfood—optional

Place all ingredients in a blender and blend until smooth and creamy. Taste and add a natural sweetener of choice if needed. Serve immediately. ↩

*Raw Vegan

■ AMAZING ELIXIRS, TONICS, AND CULTURED DRINKS

THESE AMAZING DRINKS deserve their own section. Elixirs, tonics, and cultured or fermented drinks have been used by a wide variety of different cultures for centuries. Many societies consume elixirs, tonics, and cultured or fermented drinks to help detoxify and heal the body, increase energy, increase stamina, maintain vitality, and promote good health.

I have created all of these drinks with potent superfoods that have a positive effect on the body and mind. All of the superfood ingredients can be purchased at your local health food store or online at each superfood company's Web site. Drink up and enjoy the amazing benefits that these beverages offer.

LEMON GINGER TULSI TEA

PEACH LEMONADE ELIXIR

Makes 4½ cups

I love fresh-made lemonade and sweet peaches. I decided to combine the two in this elixir with coconut water to create a really yummy and healthy elixir that you can enjoy at any time of the day. Coconut water is a very healing isotonic beverage that helps detoxify your body and is high in electrolytes, which hydrate your cells. Lemons remove toxins and add alkalinity to the body. Seek out freestone peaches, which are the best peaches for enjoying raw. Clingstone peaches are better in cooked dishes.

2 organic freestone peaches—peeled, cut in half, pits removed

3 cups young coconut water

½ cup fresh lemon juice

⅛ teaspoon or 1 packet stevia—optional

Small pinch unrefined sea salt

Place all ingredients in a blender and blend until smooth and creamy. Taste and add stevia if you like it sweeter. Chill until cold. ⌒

*Raw Vegan

E3 LIVE MELON ELIXIR

Serves 2

E3 LIVE is pure AFA blue green algae that is harvested wild from Upper Klamath Lake in Oregon. E3 live has one of the highest concentrations of protein, chlorophyll, and trace minerals of any whole food. One-half ounce provides your body with over 64 vitamins, natural chelated minerals, and living enzymes. E3 live paired with antioxidant-rich orange melon and coconut water makes a vivid green elixir that is sweet and totally original. You can purchase E3 live on their Web site or in health food stores.

2 tablespoons E3 live blue green algae (liquid or flakes)

2 cups young coconut water or filtered water

2 cups cubed peeled Sharlyn or cantaloupe melon

⅛ teaspoon or 1 packet stevia—optional

Place all ingredients in a blender and blend until smooth and creamy. Taste and add stevia if you like it sweeter. ✑

*Raw Vegan

VANILLA CARDAMOM COCONUT KEFIR

Makes 1-quart

Cultured or fermented drinks are an excellent way to enjoy healthy enzymes and probiotics which help maintain the health of our digestive system. This exotic version uses vanilla, cardamom, and coconut water but feel free to experiment with other nut or seed milks, or raw cow or goat's milk. Kefir lasts for 2 weeks in the refrigerator.

4 cups young coconut water (3 or 4 coconuts)

1 packet kefir powder

1 cinnamon stick

1 crushed green cardamom pod or ½ teaspoon ground cardamom

Vanilla bean seeds from 1 vanilla bean

1½-quart clean glass mason jar with lid

Pour warm coconut water (90°F) into a clean 1½-quart jar. Stir in kefir powder, cinnamon stick, cardamom, and vanilla bean seeds and mix until well blended. Loosely close jar and leave coconut kefir on the counter at room temperature to ferment for up to 2 days. Taste the kefir after 12 hours to see if it is ready. Kefir should be bubbly and slightly tangy. If you like the taste, screw top on securely and place in the refrigerator to lock in the flavor. Remove ¼ cup of cultured coconut kefir from the finished batch and make another batch of the recipe right away, omitting the kefir powder since you are using the actual cultured coconut kefir to ferment the new batch. Each package of the Body Ecology kefir starter will make about 6–7 (1-quart) batches.

*Raw Vegan

CINNAMON ALMOND COCONUT KEFIR

Makes 1-quart

1¾ cups unsweetened almond milk—preservative free

2¼ cups young coconut water (2 or 3 coconuts)

1 cinnamon stick

1 packet kefir powder

Pour warm almond milk and coconut water (90°F) into a clean 1½-quart jar. Stir in kefir with cinnamon stick and mix until well blended. Loosely close jar and leave on counter at room temperature to ferment for up to 2 days. Cinnamon almond coconut kefir should taste slightly tangy and bubbly. Remove ¼ cup of cultured cinnamon almond coconut kefir from the finished batch and make another batch of the recipe right away, omitting the kefir powder.

*Raw Vegan

PINEAPPLE COCONUT KEFIR

Serves 3–4

PINEAPPLES are a tropical enzyme-rich source of bromelain. Their sweet taste is wonderful blended with the tangy coconut kefir. Coconut kefir is full of live probiotics, enzymes, and electrolytes, which hydrate and keep your digestive system healthy and your body balanced. Combining the two creates a powerful elixir that is delicious and healing.

2 cups fresh pineapple—skin and core removed and cut in large chunks
3 cups vanilla cardamom coconut kefir * (recipe on page 95)
⅛ teaspoon or 1 packet stevia or 2 teaspoons raw honey

Blend pineapple with coconut kefir in a blender until smooth. Taste and add stevia or honey if you want elixir sweeter. Chill until cold. Kefir lasts for 3 days refrigerated.

*You can substitute commercial coconut water kefir if you have not made the recipe for vanilla cardamom coconut kefir. ᥓ

*Raw Vegan

CHIA MILK KEFIR

Yields around 4 cups

CHIA SEEDS are a nutritional powerhouse. In the Mayan language, chia stands for strength. These small seeds are hydrophilic, or water loving, which makes them extremely hydrating to the body. Chia seeds contain protein, calcium, magnesium, antioxidants, phytochemicals, omega-3 essential fatty acids, and soluble fiber, which make these seeds a potent superfood. When chia seeds are combined with the kefir, you get a powerful combination of live probiotics and nutrients. Drink this creamy tonic as is or use in your smoothies and salad dressings to increase the nutritional content.

3 cups organic plain unsweetened goat or cow's milk kefir
⅓ cup Chia seeds

In a 32-ounce glass jar with top, mix together all ingredients until well combined. Place in refrigerator and allow Chia seeds to gel. Use this tonic to mix in smoothies to boost the nutritional content and add a healthy source of omega-3 essential fatty acids. You can also drink the tonic by itself with a small amount of healthy sweetener added. ᥓ

CARROT ORANGE TONIC

Yields around 3½ cups

CARROTS AND ORANGES form a wonderful union when paired together. I decided to create a tonic which includes these beneficial ingredients along with the comforting and familiar flavors of ginger and cinnamon. Coconuts contain medium chain fatty acids, which our body uses for energy production. If you don't have a juicer, you can purchase fresh orange juice and carrot juice from your local juice bar or natural foods store.

1½ cups fresh carrot juice

1½ cups fresh orange juice

½ cup vanilla cardamom coconut kefir or organic unsweetened coconut milk—preservative free

1 teaspoon cinnamon

1 teaspoon fresh ginger or ¼ teaspoon organic ginger powder

⅛ teaspoon or 1 packet stevia—optional

Place all ingredients in a blender and blend until smooth and creamy. Taste and add stevia if you like the tonic sweeter. Serve cold. Tonic lasts for 2 days in the refrigerator. ↶

*Raw Vegan

HAZELNUT HERBAL COFFEE

Makes around 4 cups

TEECCINO is an herbal coffee that contains organic carob, organic barley, organic chicory, organic dates, almonds, organic figs, and inulin fiber. It tastes just like coffee without the stimulants and acidity. Teeccino comes in a wide variety of flavors to satisfy any coffee drinker's taste and preference. I personally love the hazelnut flavor and used it in this recipe. If you don't have a coffee maker, feel free to use Teeccino's tee bags. If you are a heavy coffee drinker, I recommend substituting Teeccino over a period of time to wean yourself from coffee. Start with half Teeccino, half coffee, and reduce the amount of coffee slowly until you are only using Teeccino. By doing it over a period of time, you will avoid experiencing withdrawal symptoms.

4 cups filtered or spring water

2 tablespoons Teeccino hazelnut herbal coffee

¼ teaspoon cinnamon

1 teaspoon pure vanilla extract

Unsweetened almond milk or organic half and half

Coconut sugar, Rapadura, or stevia—to taste

Place Teeccino herbal coffee grounds into the filter basket of your coffee maker. Add cinnamon on top of grounds and place vanilla extract into glass coffee maker carafe. Brew according to coffee maker's instructions. Pour into heatproof cups and add almond milk or half-and-half and sweetener of choice to taste. ↶ *Vegan

GRAPEFRUIT KOMBUCHA TEA SODA

Serves 2

KOMBUCHA TEA is made with a colony of yeast and good bacteria that is cultured or fermented with tea to produce enzymes, probiotics, lactic acid, amino acids, antioxidants, polyphenols, and glucuronic acid. Kombucha tea is healing, immune strengthening, and a great aid for your body's natural cleansing ability. I love drinking Kombucha tea whenever I'm craving a bubbly, fizzy drink. Try it as a replacement for traditional health-depleting sodas that are full of sugar or artificial sweeteners and chemicals.

1 cup ice cubes

2 cups fresh grapefruit juice

1 (16-ounce) bottle of GT Synergy or High Country Kombucha tea

Stevia—to taste

1 organic orange, lime, or lemon cut into ¼-inch slices

Place equal amounts of ice cubes into 2 tall glasses and fill each glass with 1 cup of grapefruit juice. Slowly add 8 ounces of Kombucha into each glass and add stevia to taste. Top each glass with slices of the citrus fruits of your choice. ᴄ

*Raw Vegan

SPICED MILK TEA TONIC

Serves 3

THIS SPICED MILK tea tonic is the perfect drink when you want a warm and comforting beverage. All of the ingredients blend together for an exotic, aromatic beverage filled with potent healing spices like turmeric and star anise. Turmeric's main ingredient is curcumin, which many studies have shown to have the same anti-inflammatory power as an NSAID like ibuprofen. Turmeric also gives our liver extra support and has a high amount of antioxidants, which are extremely beneficial for fighting free radicals. Puerh tea is a wonderful fermented tea that is healing to our digestive system and which the Chinese consider a healing longevity tea.

3 cups unsweetened nut or seed milk (almond, coconut, and hemp are good choices)
1 teaspoon turmeric powder or 1-inch piece fresh peeled grated turmeric root
1 star anise pod
2 Numi chocolate Puerh tea bags
Raw honey or stevia to taste

Add all ingredients except honey or stevia and tea bags in a saucepan and stir to combine. Simmer all ingredients over medium low heat until hot, but not boiling. Pour the milk into large heatproof mugs and add tea bags and allow the tea to steep for 2–3 minutes. Add honey or stevia to taste. ✑

*Vegan

LEMON GINGER TULSI TEA

Serves 2

GINGER has a spicy, warm flavor and is a well-known digestive aid, inflammation fighter, and is good for increasing circulation. Tulsi or Holy Basil is considered a sacred herb in India that is rich in phytochemicals and antioxidants. Tulsi is also an adaptogen herb renowned for reducing inflammation, increasing stamina, and relieving stress. When ginger is mixed with the tulsi tea, lemon, and raw honey, you get a tea that is sweet, warming, and energizing.

½ fresh organic lemon cut in half
2 tablespoons fresh ginger—peeled and grated
3 cups filtered or spring water
2 Organic India tulsi lemon ginger tea bags
Raw honey or stevia to taste

Squeeze lemon juice in small saucepan and add ginger. Add water and bring to a low boil. Turn down heat and allow water to simmer for 20 minutes. Remove from heat and add tulsi tea bags, allowing tea to steep for 5 minutes. Remove tea bags and strain tea into heatproof cups, adding raw honey or stevia to taste. ✑

*Vegan

BOUNTIFUL BREAKFASTS

BREAKFAST IS ONE OF MY FAVORITE MEALS OF THE DAY. I TRULY BELIEVE THAT HAVING A HEALTHY BREAKFAST GIVES YOU THE NECESSARY NUTRIENTS AND ENERGY TO START YOUR DAY OFF THE RIGHT WAY. I HAVE PROVIDED RECIPES THAT ARE QUICK AND EASY, AND SOME THAT TAKE A LITTLE MORE TIME.

COOKED BREAKFAST RECIPES ARE WONDERFUL FOR THE WEEK-ENDS OR WHEN YOU FEEL LIKED HAVING SOMETHING COOKED. ALWAYS EAT CULTURED VEGETABLES OR TAKE A PLANT-BASED EN-ZYME SUPPLEMENT WHENEVER YOU EAT COOKED FOODS TO GIVE YOUR DIGESTIVE SYSTEM ADDITIONAL SUPPORT.

THE QUICK AND EASY BREAKFASTS ARE GREAT FOR THE DAYS WHEN YOU DON'T FEEL LIKE HAVING A GREEN ENERGY SMOOTHIE FOR BREAKFAST. THESE QUICK AND EASY BREAKFASTS ARE THE PERFECT SOLUTION WHEN YOU NEED TO EAT A NUTRITIOUS MEAL ON THE GO. ALL OF THESE RECIPES CAN BE MADE IN A MATTER OF MINUTES AND WILL FILL YOU UP WITH HIGH-QUALITY NUTRITION THAT WILL KEEP YOU GOING STRONG.

FOR THE YOGURT RECIPES YOU CAN USE PLAIN GOAT'S MILK, RAW OR ORGANIC COW'S MILK, OR SHEEP'S MILK YOGURT, DEPENDING ON YOUR PERSONAL PREFERENCE AND DIETARY NEEDS. IF YOU DON'T CONSUME DAIRY, I HAVE CREATED A RECIPE FOR COCONUT YOGURT THAT YOU CAN USE AS A SUBSTITUTE FOR ANY OF THE RECIPES THAT FEATURE ANIMAL MILK-BASED YOGURT.

MANGO CHIA GINGER GRANOLA

Serves 2

Living intentions chia ginger cereal is a gluten-free, nut-free, raw vegan cereal that is made with sprouted buckwheat groats, sprouted chia seeds, sprouted quinoa, sprouted amaranth, and sprouted pumpkin seeds. It tastes like granola and is great with fresh fruit and milk. Buckwheat is an extremely nutritious seed from the buckwheat plant. Buckwheat is a source of the flavonoids quercetin and rutin, which are potent antioxidants. Buckwheat is gluten-free, high in protein, magnesium, lysine, and vitamin C. Amaranth is also a gluten-free grain that is high in protein and is a great source of the amino acid lysine. I make this breakfast in about 5 minutes and it keeps me going all morning. It is filled with key nutrients that are great for starting your day off right. You can also substitute my recipe for buckwheat fruit granola if you don't want to purchase the Living Intentions cereal.

2 ripe mangos—peeled, cored, and sliced in 1-inch cubes

2 cups Living Intentions chia ginger cereal

2 cups nut or seed milk

Place cut mango cubes, cereal, and milk in two bowls and enjoy!

*Raw Vegan

DELICIOUSLY HOLISTIC

ORANGE COCONUT YOGURT

Yields around 4 cups

COCONUT YOGURT is an excellent yogurt replacement for people who don't or can't eat dairy. It is creamy, rich, and satisfying. This version uses soft young coconut meat, which has a white outer shell and pointed top. If you don't want to crack open a coconut, have the store where you purchase the coconuts open them for you. Drain off the water and reserve to use in smoothies. Use a spoon or small spatula to scrape the meat from inside the shell. Make sure to remove any brown shell from the coconut meat before you make the yogurt. If the water inside the coconut is gray or cloudy, discard the coconut.

4 cups young coconut meat (around 4–6 coconuts)

2 tablespoons orange juice

2 teaspoons orange zest

Small pinch unrefined sea salt

Seeds from ½ of a vanilla bean or 1 teaspoon pure vanilla extract

1 teaspoon probiotic powder or dairy-free yogurt starter

Coconut sugar, honey, or stevia—to taste

Blend all ingredients except sweetener in a blender until smooth and creamy. Pour into a 1-quart sterilized glass jar and cover with lid. Let yogurt ferment at 105° F for 8 hours. I use my dehydrator for fermenting the yogurt. Once yogurt is fermented, add coconut sugar, honey, or stevia to taste. Place fermented yogurt covered in the refrigerator for up to 5 days.

HELPFUL TIP FOR USING PROBIOTICS IN YOUR YOGURT

Adding the probiotics will provide your coconut yogurt with beneficial bacteria. If you use probiotic capsules open them and pour into a 1 teaspoon measuring spoon to get the 1 teaspoon of powder.

---

* Raw Vegan

DELICIOUSLY HOLISTIC

BERRIES AND CREAM

Serves 2

I personally love fresh berries with raw cream, so I decided to create a version that uses seed or nut butter to satisfy the people who don't or can't eat dairy products. This version is sweet and creamy. I use nut or seed milks that are the same type as the nut or seed butter I use when I make it. Seed or nut cream also makes a wonderful ice cream. I like to blend it with fresh fruit and freeze in my ice cream maker.

3 cups of your favorite fresh organic berries

½ cup seed or nut cream—recipe follows

In each of two serving dishes, place 1½ cups of fresh berries and ¼ cup of seed or nut cream.

RAW SEED OR NUT CREAM

½ cup sprouted or raw nut or seed butter (pecan, walnut, almond, pumpkin, and sunflower seed are good choices)

⅓ cup unsweetened nut or seed milk

1 tablespoon pure vanilla extract or seeds from 1 vanilla bean

¼ teaspoon cinnamon

⅓ cup coconut sugar or coconut nectar, or ¼ teaspoon stevia

Place all ingredients in a small bowl and blend with a spoon until creamy and smooth. If cream is too thick, add additional milk 1 tablespoon at a time. Taste and add more sweetener if you like the cream sweeter.

*Raw Vegan

PEAR POMEGRANATE NUT BOWL

Serves 2

PEARS AND POMEGRANATES are two of my favorite fruits. I love the sweet and juicy, lush bites of the pear contrasted with the sweet and tangy bite of the ruby red pomegranate seeds and creamy pecan butter. Pomegranates are a great source of the phytochemical ellagic acid a potent antioxidant. This fruit and nut bowl is very satisfying and a great way to start your day with a wonderful balance of protein, vitamins, minerals, fiber, and healthy fats.

2 large organic pears*—rinsed, dried, cored, and cut in half

½ cup sprouted or raw pecan butter

1 teaspoon fresh ginger—peeled and grated

1 teaspoon cinnamon

2 teaspoons pure vanilla extract

3 tablespoons coconut sugar or ⅛ teaspoon stevia

⅓ cup dried unsweetened coconut flakes

½ cup pomegranate seeds

½ cup buckwheat fruit granola—optional (recipe on page 115)

Slice pears halves into quarters and combine with nut butter, ginger, cinnamon, vanilla, your choice of sweetener, and coconut flakes in food processor with S blade. Process until chunky and combined together. Place in bowls and top with pomegranate seeds and buckwheat fruit granola if using.

HELPFUL TIP FOR REMOVING POMEGRANATE SEEDS

Cut pomegranate in half. Place a bowl in front of you and hold the cut side of the pomegranate half down. Hit the back of the pomegranate half with a large spoon until all the seeds fall out into the bowl. Discard the white pith and outer skin.

---

*Choose your favorite pear. I love Red Anjou pears, Bartlett pears, or Comice pears.

*Raw Vegan

NECTARINE YOGURT PARFAIT

Serves 2

FRESH FRUIT AND YOGURT are an excellent way to enjoy a healthy, quick breakfast that features phytonutrients, vitamins, minerals, live probiotics, fiber, and nourishing fats. Peaches and berries are also great in this parfait. Feel free to substitute your favorite fruits that are in season.

1½ cups organic plain Greek yogurt or orange coconut yogurt

1 tablespoon lemon juice

1 teaspoon pure vanilla extract

½ teaspoon cinnamon

2 tablespoons coconut sugar, coconut nectar or maple syrup

2 large organic nectarines—rinsed, dried, pitted, and cut into ½-inch cubes

¼ cup sprouted or raw nuts or seeds, or buckwheat fruit granola (recipe on page 115)

In medium-size bowl, blend together yogurt, lemon juice, vanilla extract, cinnamon, and sweetener of choice. If using coconut yogurt, omit the lemon juice. Taste yogurt and add more sweetener if you like. Place 2 parfait or martini glasses on counter and place ¼ cup of nectarine cubes on bottom of each glass, add a layer of yogurt, and repeat the process until you almost reach the top. Sprinkle with raw nuts or seeds or buckwheat granola.

■ COOKED BREAKFASTS

I USUALLY ENJOY COOKED BREAKFASTS on the weekends, when I have extra time, or when I have brunch with friends. I love eggs and vegetables together, so I have included some of my favorite recipes that feature these ingredients. Feel free to substitute your favorite seasonal vegetables in any of the egg recipes.

Pastured eggs are a great, economical source of omega-3 essential fatty acids, protein, lutein, beta-carotene, choline, vitamin K, vitamin E, vitamin A, and B vitamins. Pastured eggs have less cholesterol and saturated fat than eggs from factory-farm-raised chickens. The yolks of pastured eggs are deep yellow, and the flavor of these eggs is far better than factory-farmed eggs. Pastured eggs come from pasture-raised chickens that have been allowed to roam freely outdoors and eat a natural diet of insects and forage.

My mom loved to make French toast with me when I was growing up, and it was one of my favorite breakfasts, so I came up with my new version that features sprouted or naturally fermented organic whole grain bread that is full of nutrients and easier for the body to digest versus traditional breads made with refined and enriched flours and corn syrup.

I have included my favorite recipe for granola made with buckwheat groats, which are great gluten-free seeds that taste delicious and are very nutritious.

As a reminder, try to consume all cooked foods with cultured vegetables or plant-based enzymes to give your digestive system additional support.

CRANBERRY QUINOA CEREAL

Makes 2 servings

QUINOA MAKES A WONDERFUL hot breakfast cereal that is high in protein and will give you energy to perform your morning activities easily. I love this comforting cereal especially in the winter months when I want something warm and delicious to start the day with. This cereal features Zhena's Gypsy Tea Ambrosia Plum, an antioxidant-rich, exotic blend of rare white Assam and Indian green tea, plum, strawberry leaves, and delicate rose. This fair-trade tea adds an exotic, sweet flavor to the quinoa cereal. I like using teas in unique ways to add additional key nutrients and layers of flavor. If you don't have the tea, make the cereal without it, because it also good that way. Be sure to soak your quinoa at room temperature overnight in enough filtered water to cover it, and add 2 tablespoons of fresh lemon juice to the water to remove the anti-nutrients in the quinoa.

2 cups filtered water

1– Zhena's Gypsy Tea Ambrosia Plum tea sachet

1 cup quinoa—soaked overnight in lemon water, rinsed and drained

1 teaspoon cinnamon

2 teaspoons pure vanilla extract

Small pinch unrefined sea salt

¼ cup nut or seed milk, coconut milk, or organic cream—optional to top cereal

½ cup dried unsulfured cranberries

2 tablespoons raw honey

¼ cup sprouted or raw walnuts

Heat 2 cups of filtered water over medium high heat in a small saucepan. Once water gets very hot but before it boils, add tea sachet and steep on the stovetop for 3 minutes. Lightly squeeze tea sachet into pot after steeping and remove. Add rinsed quinoa, cinnamon, vanilla, and sea salt to pot and stir well. Cover pot and simmer quinoa on medium heat for around 15 minutes until liquid is absorbed and quinoa is tender. Stir quinoa and spoon into bowls. Drizzle with milk or cream if desired and top with cranberries, honey, and walnuts. ᴥ

*Vegan

DELICIOUSLY HOLISTIC

FRENCH TOAST WITH SPICED BLUEBERRY SYRUP

Serves 4

BLUEBERRIES are one of my favorite superfood fruits, so I try to find new ways to use them in my recipes. This French toast is packed with nutrition and tastes so good with the spiced blueberry syrup!

1 cup fresh wild or organic blueberries, or frozen, defrosted

½ cup plus 2 tablespoons spiced maple syrup (recipe on page 57)

1½ cups unsweetened almond milk or organic cow's milk

2 large eggs

1 teaspoon cinnamon

2 teaspoons pure vanilla extract

8 slices whole grain sourdough or sprouted bread

4–5 tablespoons virgin coconut oil or organic clarified butter

In small saucepan mix together blueberries and ½ cup spiced maple syrup and cook over medium heat for around 20 minutes until blueberries burst and release their juice, forming a blueberry syrup. Stir syrup occasionally while cooking. Remove from heat, cover, and set syrup aside while you make the French toast. Preheat oven to 200° F. In large mixing bowl, whisk together milk, eggs, cinnamon, vanilla extract, and 2 tablespoons spiced maple syrup. Pour this mixture into a shallow rectangular dish. Use a fork to poke several holes in bread so that the egg custard can absorb easily. Dip both sides of bread into egg mixture and allow mixture to soak in for 3–5 minutes. Heat 2 tablespoons of the coconut oil or clarified butter on medium heat in a large frying pan. Don't allow oil to overheat! Place 2 or 3 pieces of French toast in pan and cook for 3 or 4 minutes on each side until golden brown. Place cooked pieces in oven on a baking sheet pan and keep warm while cooking remaining slices of French toast. Serve French toast with spiced blueberry maple syrup. ~

DELICIOUSLY HOLISTIC

BUCKWHEAT FRUIT GRANOLA

Yields around 11 cups

This is a great recipe to make on the weekends when you have more time to soak the buckwheat groats and bake the granola. This recipe is my favorite, but you can use whatever combination of dried fruits and nuts or seeds that you have on hand. Buckwheat is an extremely nutritious seed from the buckwheat plant. Buckwheat is a good source of the flavonoids quercetin and rutin, which are potent antioxidants. Buckwheat is gluten-free, high in protein, magnesium, and vitamin C. You can find buckwheat groats in most natural food markets in the bulk bins.

4 cups buckwheat groats

¼ cup fresh lemon juice or raw apple cider vinegar

¼ cup melted virgin coconut oil

1 cup organic maple syrup—grade B

2 tablespoons pure vanilla extract

2 teaspoons cinnamon

1½ teaspoons sea salt

½ cup dried white mulberries

½ cup dried unsulfured golden and dark raisins

½ cup dried goji berries

1½ cups sprouted or raw pistachios

½ cup sprouted or raw pumpkin seeds

1 cup unsweetened large coconut flakes

Place buckwheat groats in a large mixing bowl with lemon juice or vinegar and enough water to cover. Soak at room temperature for 8 hours or overnight. Rinse and drain well. Place groats in the bowl of food processor fitted with the S blade and pulse until chunky but not completely pureed. In saucepan over low heat melt coconut oil and mix with maple syrup, vanilla, cinnamon, and sea salt. Pour over buckwheat groats and mix thoroughly. Spread groats on parchment-lined sheet pans and place in a 200° F oven and bake for several hours until dry and crispy. If you have a dehydrator, spread groats onto nonstick sheets and dehydrate at 115° F for 10 hours. Flip buckwheat groats onto mesh screens and continue drying for 2–3 more hours until dry and crispy. Remove buckwheat from oven or dehydrator, break into small pieces, and mix with mulberries, raisins, goji berries, pistachios, pumpkin seeds, and coconut flakes. Store the granola in an airtight container. Granola will last for several months. ☙

*Vegan

DELICIOUSLY HOLISTIC

BUTTERMILK MILLET WAFFLES

Makes 4–6 waffles depending on waffle iron size

BUTTERMILK WAFFLES are the quintessential breakfast food. I don't know of anyone who doesn't like a hot, crispy waffle dripping with maple syrup or covered in fresh fruits. I created these waffles for gluten-free eaters who miss having traditional waffles. These waffles are much better for you because they are made without refined, bleached, white flour, which is low in nutrients. The millet makes a yummy, nutty-tasting waffle that has a wonderful, crisp texture. To Your Health Sprouted Flour Company or Blue Mountain Organics are good choices for sprouted millet flour and Arrowhead Mills for organic unsprouted millet flour.

2 large eggs—yolks and whites separated

¾–1 cup organic buttermilk

2 teaspoons pure vanilla extract

2 tablespoons melted virgin coconut oil or melted organic unsalted butter

1¼ cups organic sprouted or regular millet flour

¼ teaspoon unrefined sea salt

1½ teaspoons cinnamon

2 teaspoons baking powder—aluminum free

1 tablespoon coconut sugar or Rapadura

Organic virgin coconut oil to grease waffle iron

To serve—spiced maple syrup and organic unsalted butter at room temperature

Heat waffle iron on high. Beat egg whites with wire whisk or electric mixer until firm peaks form, then set aside. In small mixing bowl whisk together ¾ cup buttermilk, egg yolks, vanilla extract, and melted cooled coconut oil or butter, then set aside. In medium-size mixing bowl, stir together millet flour, sea salt, cinnamon, baking powder, and coconut sugar or Rapadura thoroughly. Slowly pour liquid ingredients into dry ingredients and mix until combined. Add additional ¼ cup of buttermilk if needed. Fold egg whites gently into waffle batter. Grease waffle iron with coconut oil. Pour around ¼ cup–½ cup of batter into waffle iron and spread evenly to the edge. Close lid and cook waffles until golden brown and steam stops; it should take around 3 to 5 minutes depending on the waffle iron. Remove waffle with fork and serve immediately with butter and spiced maple syrup. ⌒

CHAI PUMPKIN OATMEAL

Makes 2 servings

I LOVE CHAI TEA, oatmeal, and pumpkin, so I decided to combine them in this recipe. The result is a nutrient-rich, creamy, sweet, and satisfying hot oatmeal which is perfect to enjoy on a chilly day. This recipe features Zhena's Gypsy Tea Fire Light Chai, an antioxidant-rich, caffeine-free Rooibos tea with the exotic spices of ginger, cinnamon, cardamom, and clove. Oatmeal and pumpkin are good sources of fiber, and the chai tea adds an unexpected flavor note that blends perfectly with the pumpkin. Soaking the oatmeal overnight in filtered water mixed with 2 tablespoons of lemon juice removes the phytic acid in the oats, which makes the oats easier to digest and more nutritious.

1 cup filtered water

1 cup coconut milk plus 2 tablespoons for topping oatmeal

2 teaspoons pure vanilla extract

¼ teaspoon unrefined sea salt

Zhena's Gypsy Tea Fire Light Chai—use 2 teaspoons of loose-leaf tea or 1 tea sachet

3 tablespoons organic maple syrup—grade B

¾ cup cooked pumpkin purée

1 cup rolled oats—soaked overnight in lemon water, rinsed and drained

¼ cup white mulberries or golden raisins

¼ cup chopped sprouted or raw walnuts—optional

Cinnamon to taste

In medium saucepan, mix together water, coconut milk, vanilla, and sea salt. Bring mixture to a simmer on medium heat. Once coconut water is hot but not boiling, either place tea leaves in a tea ball or add tea sachet to coconut water and steep for 3–5 minutes. The longer you steep the tea, the more intense the chai flavor will be. After steeping, remove tea and stir in maple syrup, pumpkin purée, and drained rolled oats. Cover and cook over medium heat for around 10 minutes, stirring occasionally, until thick and creamy and oats are soft and hot. Remove oatmeal from heat and spoon into two bowls. Top with coconut milk, mulberries or raisins, walnuts if using, and cinnamon. Taste and drizzle with more maple syrup if you want your oatmeal sweeter.

*Vegan

BASIC GRITS

Serves 4

GRITS ARE A SOUTHERN STAPLE. You can't have a good southern breakfast without including grits on the menu! I use corn stock in my grits to intensify the sweet corn flavor, but if you don't make my recipe for corn stock, feel free to use water. My favorite way to eat grits is with cultured butter, sea salt, and pepper. My grandfather likes his with cream. After making the basic grits, you can decide what suits your taste.

4–5 cups corn stock or filtered water (recipe on page 130)

1 teaspoon unrefined sea salt

1 cup organic corn grits (stone ground or regular)

Heat 4 cups of corn stock or water in medium-size saucepan with sea salt until boiling. Stir in grits, making sure there are no lumps. Cover pan with lid, reduce heat to low, and simmer for 25 minutes for regular grits or 45 to 60 minutes for stone ground grits, until thick and creamy, stirring frequently to avoid lumps. Add additional stock or water if needed. Serve with butter, sea salt, and fresh ground black pepper. ✎

BALSAMIC BROWN BUTTER GRITS

Serves 4

This recipe for grits is a little more decadent than regular grits because they are drizzled with a nutty and slightly tangy balsamic brown butter sauce.

⅓ cup organic unsalted butter

2 tablespoons balsamic vinegar

Unrefined sea salt and fresh ground black pepper

1 recipe for basic grits

Melt butter in a small saucepan over low heat until the butter turns golden and smells nutty. Be careful not to burn butter! Remove pan from stove and slowly stir in balsamic vinegar. Place back on stove and cook for 1 minute longer. Stir in sea salt and black pepper to taste. Drizzle a small amount of balsamic brown butter over hot cooked grits and serve immediately. ✎

GREEN LEAF LETTUCE, TOMATO, AND ONION SCRAMBLE

Serves 3

PASTURED EGGS are full of nutrients that are good for you because the chickens are allowed to eat a natural diet of forage and insects and they get exercise, fresh air, and sunshine daily. This diet produces eggs that have a deep yellow yolk and are high in vitamin D, vitamin A, protein, vitamin K, lutein, and omega-3 fatty acids. Adding the tomatoes and green leaf lettuce adds a healthy dose of nutrients like vitamin C, lycopene, and chlorophyll, as well as delicate onion flavor from the white onions. Green leaf lettuce tastes wonderful when lightly sautéed. Make sure to stop cooking the eggs when they are still shiny and wet looking to avoid drying them out. I love raw goat's milk cheese in this scramble, but feel free to use your favorite cheese.

1 tablespoon organic unsalted butter or olive oil

½ cup roma tomatoes—cut into ½-inch cubes

1 cup shredded organic green oak leaf lettuce—rinsed thoroughly and patted dry

¼ cup peeled chopped white onion

6 large eggs

⅓ cup raw goat's milk cheese—shredded or cut into small cubes

⅛ cup filtered water

1 teaspoon unrefined sea salt

Fresh ground black pepper to taste

Heat the butter or olive oil in a sauté pan or skillet over medium heat until hot but not smoking. Swirl butter or olive oil around in pan and add tomatoes, shredded lettuce, and onion; sprinkle with sea salt and black pepper to taste and cook, stirring occasionally, until soft. While vegetables are cooking, get eggs ready. Break eggs into a medium bowl. Add cheese, water, 1 teaspoon of sea salt, and pepper; whip eggs with fork until bubbles form, then set aside. Reduce heat to medium low and pour egg mixture on top of cooked vegetables. Using a heat-resistant spoon or spatula, move eggs toward center of pan and lift and fold eggs until they form a mound of creamy and shiny eggs. This should take around 2 or 3 minutes. Remove eggs and serve immediately.

* If you have dairy intolerances, leave out the cheese and make the eggs with vegetables only.

DELICIOUSLY HOLISTIC

RAINBOW CHARD OMELET

Serves 2

AN OMELET is a sophisticated way to serve eggs. There are so many variations you can create, so I decided to make an omelet featuring rainbow or red chard. Rainbow or red chard is a vividly colored, leafy green vegetable with a sweet flavor and tender texture. Rainbow or red chard is a potent cancer-fighting food that is a good source of carotenes, vitamin K, magnesium, calcium, chlorophyll, and soluble fiber. Reserve the stems to use in vegetable stock.

2 cups thinly sliced rainbow or red chard (remove stems before slicing)

⅓ cup filtered water

5 teaspoons organic unsalted butter or virgin coconut oil

¼ cup peeled diced white onion

Unrefined sea salt to taste

Fresh ground black pepper to taste

¼ teaspoon garlic powder—optional

5 large eggs

1 tablespoon filtered water or organic milk

⅓ cup raw milk cheese—shredded

In a 10-inch skillet or omelet pan add shredded chard, ⅓ cup of water, 1 teaspoon butter or coconut oil, and diced white onion. Season the chard to taste with sea salt, black pepper, and garlic powder, if using; cover and cook on medium heat until wilted and tender, stirring occasionally. Place chard on a plate and cover to keep warm while you make the 2 omelets. Whisk the eggs in a bowl with sea salt, black pepper, and water or milk. Wipe out pan which had the chard, add 2 teaspoons of butter or coconut oil to the pan, and heat over medium heat until butter or coconut oil gets hot but doesn't smoke. Pour ½ of the eggs into pan and let eggs set for about 20 seconds and lift edges with heat-resistant spatula, tilting pan to allow runny part of the egg to go under omelet and cook. Place ½ of the cooked chard and sprinkle with half the cheese on 1 side of the omelet. Omelet should be firm but still be shiny and moist on top. Jerk pan to loosen omelet and fold over in half. Remove from heat and slide omelet onto a serving plate. Repeat process for next omelet. Serve immediately. ⌒

* If you have dairy intolerances, leave out cheese and make the eggs with vegetables only.

CARAMELIZED BALSAMIC ONION SCRAMBLE

Serves 3

I love creating different recipes for scrambled eggs. This recipe uses yellow onions cooked with balsamic vinegar, which adds a sweet and tangy note which is wonderful with the creamy eggs. If you have white or red onions, you can still make the recipe. Onions are a member of the allium family and are a good source of nutrients like chromium, which helps balance blood sugar, and sulfur, which is an anti-aging mineral. Onions are also a potent cancer fighter.

3 tablespoons organic unsalted butter or virgin coconut oil

2 peeled medium yellow onions—thinly sliced

½ teaspoon unrefined sea salt—for onions

1 teaspoon coconut sugar or Rapadura

2 tablespoons balsamic vinegar

6 large eggs

⅛ cup filtered water

Unrefined sea salt to taste

Fresh ground black pepper to taste

Melt 2 tablespoons of butter or coconut oil in a sauté pan or skillet on medium heat and add onions. Sprinkle onions with ½ teaspoon sea salt, sweetener of choice, and balsamic vinegar and cook for around 30 minutes until onions become soft, caramelized, and golden brown. Stir onions occasionally while cooking. Remove onions from stove and cover to keep warm. In bowl, whip eggs with water, sea salt, and black pepper to taste. Rinse and dry pan which held onions, place on stove, and melt 1 tablespoon butter or coconut oil over medium-low heat in pan. Pour beaten eggs in pan and, with heat-resistant spatula or spoon, move eggs toward center of pan, then lift and fold eggs over until they form a mound of creamy, shiny eggs. This should take around 2 or 3 minutes. Remove eggs from heat while still slightly wet and shiny. Top with onions and serve immediately. ⌐

YELLOW SQUASH AND BASIL OMELET

Serves 2

YELLOW SQUASH is a bright yellow summer squash that has a mild taste that pairs nicely with the eggs and fresh basil. Both zucchini and yellow squash are healing foods for the liver. The green onion adds another layer of flavor and adds additional important vitamins, minerals, and fiber.

6 teaspoons organic unsalted clarified butter

1½ cups diced yellow squash

½ cup chopped green onions

2 cloves peeled garlic—grated

6 fresh basil leaves—torn into small pieces

Unrefined sea salt to taste

Fresh ground black pepper to taste

5 large eggs

1 tablespoon filtered water or organic milk

Heat 2 teaspoons of clarified butter in a 10-inch skillet or omelet pan over medium-high heat. Add the yellow squash, green onion, garlic, and basil leaves and season to taste with sea salt and black pepper. Cook until squash is soft but not mushy. Place vegetables on a plate and cover to keep warm while you make the 2 omelets. Whisk the eggs in a bowl with sea salt and black pepper to taste, and water or milk. Wipe out pan which had the vegetables with a paper towel, add 2 teaspoons of clarified butter to the pan, and heat over medium heat until butter gets hot but doesn't smoke. Pour in ½ the eggs and let eggs sit for about 20 seconds, lifting edges with heat-resistant spatula, tilting pan to allow runny part of the egg to go under the omelet and cook. Place ½ the squash mixture on 1 side of the omelet and continue cooking until omelet is firm but still shiny and moist on top. Jerk pan to loosen omelet and fold in half. Repeat process for next omelet. Serve immediately. ✎

SATISFYING SOUPS AND STOCKS

I LOVE SOUPS. THEY ARE VERY SATISFYING AND ARE A PERFECT START TO A MEAL OR WONDERFUL AS A MAIN COURSE. I HAVE INCLUDED RECIPES FOR BOTH COOKED AND RAW SOUPS AS WELL AS BEEF, CHICKEN, AND VEGETABLE STOCKS, WHICH FORM THE BASIS OF GREAT SOUPS AND SAUCES. I MAKE STOCKS IN THE SLOW COOKER OR ON THE STOVETOP ONCE OR TWICE A MONTH, DEPENDING ON HOW BUSY I AM, AND FREEZE IN DIFFERENT SIZE STORAGE CONTAINERS TO USE IN RECIPES OR CONSUME AS IS. BEEF OR CHICKEN STOCK AKA BONE BROTH IS MINERAL-RICH AND HEALING TO THE BODY. STOCK OR BONE BROTH CONTAINS GELATIN, WHICH IS HYDROPHILIC (WATER LOVING), AND HELPS TO KEEP THE MUCOSAL LINING OF OUR INTESTINES HEALTHY.

ENJOYING STOCKS OR BROTHS REGULARLY CAN HELP IMPROVE YOUR DIGESTION AND BOOST YOUR IMMUNE SYSTEM. ALWAYS COOL YOUR STOCKS AND HOT SOUPS DOWN QUICKLY TO KEEP THEM OUT OF THE DANGER TEMPERATURE ZONE WHERE BAD BACTERIA GROW. THE TEMPERATURE YOU WANT TO AVOID IS 40° F–140° F. BY COOLING PROPERLY BEFORE STORING IN THE REFRIGERATOR, YOU ALSO PREVENT OTHER FOODS IN YOUR REFRIGERATOR FROM GETTING IN THE DANGER ZONE.

WHEN YOU EAT THE STOCK BY ITSELF, MAKE SURE TO SEASON TO TASTE WITH A SMALL AMOUNT OF UNREFINED SEA SALT, SUCH AS CELTIC OR HIMALAYAN, BEFORE ENJOYING. IF USING STOCK AS THE BASE FOR OTHER SOUP RECIPES, FOLLOW DIRECTIONS IN THE RECIPE FOR ADDING SALT.

CHICKEN STOCK

Makes around 2½ quarts

1 whole 3½-pound pasture-raised or organic chicken or 4-pounds chicken wings

½ cup dry white wine

3 quarts filtered water (12 cups)

1 large white onion—peeled and coarsely chopped

3 large organic carrots—peeled and coarsely chopped

4 organic celery ribs—coarsely chopped

8 fresh parsley sprigs

3 fresh thyme sprigs

½ teaspoon black peppercorns

2 bay leaves

3 cloves peeled garlic

If using a whole chicken, you can have the butcher cut it into pieces and give you the neck also, or cut it yourself. If cutting yourself, remove neck, liver, and gizzards. Place chicken pieces and neck or chicken wings in large stockpot with wine and water. Let stock sit for 20 minutes before cooking. Bring to a boil over high heat; turn heat to low and skim off foam that rises to the top. Add the vegetables, herbs, black peppercorns, bay leaves, and garlic to the stockpot. Partially cover pot and maintain a low simmer for 6–10 hours. The stock will become more nutrient-dense if cooked for a longer period of time. Skim occasionally if needed. When done, remove chicken from stock with slotted spoon. Strain stock through a mesh strainer into a large, heatproof bowl, pushing down on solids with a large spoon to extract maximum flavor. Place bowl of hot stock in a sink of ice and cold water to chill down quickly. Stir stock occasionally to release heat. Refrigerate in several covered containers for up to 4 days. Skim fat off top before using. You can store stock in refrigerator for additional 2 days if you bring stock back to a boil. You can also freeze the stock in covered containers for 4–6 months.

ROASTED CHICKEN STOCK

Season chicken pieces or wings with sea salt to taste. Place in a roasting pan and bake at 400° F for 45 minutes until golden brown. Turn once or twice to ensure even browning. Place in stockpot and follow the recipe for chicken stock.

BEEF STOCK

Makes around 3½ quarts

3-pounds grass-fed organic beef neck bones or beef shanks

3-pounds meaty grass-fed organic beef marrow and knuckle bones

1 large white onion—peeled and cut in half

1 head garlic—cut in half crosswise

3 organic carrots—peeled and coarsely chopped

4 organic celery ribs—coarsely chopped

½ cup dry red wine

2 tablespoons organic tomato paste

4 quarts filtered water (16 cups)

10 fresh parsley sprigs

6 fresh thyme sprigs

2 bay leaves

1 teaspoon black peppercorns

Place neck bones or shanks, marrow bones, and knuckle bones in a large roasting pan with onions and garlic halves. Roast in the oven at 375° F for around 40 minutes. When browned, add meat bones, onions, and garlic to stockpot with carrots and celery. Drain fat out of roasting pan, add red wine and tomato paste to the roasting pan, and stir with wooden spoon to loosen up brown bits. Add this to stockpot. Add enough water to cover bones, but don't let liquid go higher than 2 inches from top of stockpot. Let stock sit for around 20 minutes before cooking. Bring stock to a boil; turn down heat to low, and skim foam from the top with a large spoon. Add parsley, thyme, bay leaves, and black peppercorns to stock. Simmer stock on low partially covered for 8–12 hours, skimming occasionally if needed. The stock will become more nutrient-dense if simmered for a longer period of time. When done, remove bones and strain stock through a mesh strainer into a large heatproof bowl, pressing down on solids with a spoon to extract maximum flavor. Place bowl in sink full of ice and cold water to cool stock down quickly. Stir occasionally to release heat. Place cooled stock into several covered storage containers and place in refrigerator for up to 4 days. Skim fat off the top before using. You can store stock in refrigerator for additional 2 days if you bring stock back to a boil. You can also freeze the stock in covered containers for 4–6 months.

VEGETABLE STOCK

Makes around 3½ quarts

Vegetable stock is great for people who don't eat meat-based stocks or broths. Feel free to substitute this stock in any of my recipes that use chicken or beef stock. The organic potato skins and onion skins add additional minerals and nutrients to the stock.

3 tablespoons extra virgin olive oil

3 large organic carrots—peeled and chopped

2 large unpeeled organic red onions—chopped (reserve outer skins)

1 cup cremini mushrooms—cleaned and chopped

5 stalks organic celery with tops—chopped

3 cups organic potato skins

3 cloves peeled garlic

½ cup white wine

4 quarts filtered water (16 cups)

2 bay leaves

2 teaspoons unrefined sea salt

10 fresh parsley sprigs

4 fresh thyme sprigs

½ teaspoon black peppercorns

Pour olive oil into large stockpot over medium heat and add carrots, onions, mushrooms, and celery. Cook over medium heat until soft, stirring occasionally. Add potato skins, garlic, white wine, water, bay leaves, sea salt, parsley, thyme, black peppercorns, and reserved onion skins. Bring to a boil. Skim off any foam. Turn heat down to low and partially cover. Simmer stock for 45 minutes to 1 hour. Strain stock with mesh strainer into large heatproof bowl, pressing down on solids with a large spoon to extract maximum flavor. Cool down bowl of stock in a sink filled with ice and cold water. Stir occasionally to release heat. Stock will last for 4 days covered in the refrigerator and 3 months in the freezer.

*Vegan

CORN STOCK

Makes around 2½ quarts

I love to make corn stock when corn is in season and plentiful. Sweet corn makes a wonderful light stock that can be used in a variety of different recipes or enjoyed as is. Use the corn kernels to make my recipe for corn soup or freeze them for later use.

10 cobs organic yellow corn—kernels removed and broken into smaller pieces

1 bay leaf

2 teaspoons unrefined sea salt

3 fresh thyme sprigs

½ head garlic

4 black peppercorns

⅛ teaspoon vanilla beans or ¼ teaspoon pure vanilla extract

10 cups filtered water

Place all ingredients in a large stockpot and bring to a boil on medium-high heat. Skim foam off top and reduce heat to low. Simmer corn stock partially covered for 1 hour. Strain stock through a mesh strainer into large heatproof containers, pressing down on solids with a large spoon to extract maximum flavor. Place containers in sink filled with ice and water to cool quickly. Stir occasionally to release heat. Stock will last for 4 days covered in the refrigerator and 3 months in the freezer.

*Vegan

TOMATO BASIL CREAM SOUP

Makes around 2–3 servings

When I was a little girl, creamy tomato soup was my absolute favorite soup, and it still is today. I use fresh tomatoes when in season or substitute organic tomatoes by Eden Foods when fresh tomatoes are not at their peak. Cooked tomatoes are a good source of lycopene, which is a carotene that protects the body against a wide variety of cancers. Lycopene is absorbed better in the presence of fat. Tomatoes also provide vitamin C, folic acid, and vitamin K.

2 tablespoons virgin coconut oil or organic unsalted butter

½ cup peeled chopped white onion

3 cloves peeled garlic—grated

4 teaspoons organic tomato paste

4 large beefsteak tomatoes—remove skin and seeds and chop (4 cups)

4 cups organic chicken stock or vegetable stock

2 or 3 tablespoons coconut sugar

2 teaspoons unrefined sea salt (adjust amount of sea salt if using commercial stock)

½ teaspoon fresh ground black pepper

⅓ cup organic cream

¼ cup chopped fresh basil leaves

⅓ cup chopped oven-dried tomatoes (recipe on page 60)

In medium-size stockpot, melt coconut oil or butter over medium heat, and add onions. Cook onions until soft, around 5 minutes. Add garlic and tomato paste during last 2 minutes of onions cooking. Add chopped tomatoes, stock, 2 tablespoons of coconut sugar, sea salt, and black pepper. Stir and bring to a boil. Reduce heat to simmer and cook partially covered for around 30 minutes. Add cream and simmer on low for an additional 10–15 minutes. Taste soup and add additional sweetener if needed. Puree hot soup with immersion blender until smooth. If you use a regular blender, blend soup in small batches and place a towel on blender top, holding down firmly so the hot soup doesn't pop out of the blender and burn you. Taste and adjust seasoning. Pour into serving bowls, sprinkle with basil leaves and chopped oven-dried tomatoes, and serve immediately.

VEGAN VERSION: use coconut oil, vegetable stock, and unsweetened nut or seed milk.

PUMPKIN HAZELNUT CHAI SOUP

Makes 4 servings

Pumpkin is a wonderful winter squash. It is a versatile superstar vegetable that is good in both savory and sweet recipes. Pumpkin is a great healing vegetable to include in your diet on a regular basis because it has an exceptional amount of nutrients including carotenoids, potassium, B vitamins, vitamin C, vitamin E, magnesium, and fiber. The tea I used to create a flavor-filled tea stock for the soup base is Zhena's Gypsy Tea Hazelnut Chai Red Tea. This aromatic tea adds wonderful notes of exotic spice with its unique blend of organic Rooibos, roasted Viennese hazelnuts, cinnamon, ginger root, licorice root, cloves, cardamom, nutmeg, black pepper, and vanilla bean. In this recipe feel free to use either fresh or canned pumpkin purée.

2½ cups organic unsweetened coconut milk—preservative free

1½ cups spring or filtered water

1 teaspoon peeled, grated ginger root

2—Zhena's Gypsy Tea Hazelnut Chai Red Tea sachets

4 cups fresh roasted pumpkin purée or 2—15 ounce cans organic pumpkin purée

2 tablespoons organic maple syrup—grade B

Unrefined sea salt—to taste

½ cup sprouted or raw dried fruit and nut trail mix—optional (reserve to top soup with)

In medium-size saucepan, heat coconut milk, water, and ginger over medium heat until mixture starts to simmer but not boil. Once mixture is hot add the tea sachets and stir. Turn heat to low and let tea steep for 3–5 minutes. Remove tea sachets and blend in pumpkin purée, maple syrup, and sea salt to taste. Heat soup over medium-low heat until hot and flavors have a chance to blend together, for around 30 minutes. Stir soup occasionally. Place hot soup in serving bowls and sprinkle with trail mix if using. Enjoy immediately!

HELPFUL TIP FOR ROASTING FRESH PUMPKIN

To roast fresh pumpkin, remove the stem. Split the pumpkin in half lengthwise. Remove all of the seeds and stringy parts. Lightly drizzle with melted coconut oil or olive oil and place cut side down on a greased or non-stick baking sheet. Roast at 400° F for 45 minutes to an hour, depending on the size of the pumpkin. The pumpkin is done when the skin and flesh of the pumpkin is tender when pierced with a fork. Use puréed pumpkin flesh in the recipe.

*Vegan

SWEET POTATO MAPLE SOUP

Serves 3–4

MAPLE SYRUP adds a wonderful sweetness and depth of flavor to this comforting sweet potato soup. The sweet potato makes this soup a rich source of beta-carotene, iron, calcium, and fiber and the coconut milk adds lauric acid and creaminess to the mix.

2 tablespoons avocado or extra virgin olive oil

1 small white onion—peeled and coarsely chopped

2 organic celery ribs—coarsely chopped

⅓ cup fino sherry

4 cups orange flesh sweet potatoes—peeled and cut into 1-inch cubes

5 cups organic vegetable stock

2 tablespoons organic maple syrup—grade B

1 teaspoon cinnamon

½ teaspoon smoked sweet paprika

1 teaspoon unrefined sea salt

¼ teaspoon fresh ground black pepper

⅓ cup organic unsweetened coconut milk—preservative free

¼ cup sliced green onions

In large saucepan over medium heat add avocado oil or olive oil, white onion, and celery and cook until slightly soft around 3–4 minutes. Add cubed sweet potatoes and deglaze pan with sherry, cooking an additional 10 minutes. Add remaining ingredients except green onions and stir to combine well. Simmer over medium heat for around 30 minutes or until sweet potatoes are soft. Puree soup with hand held immersion blender. If you use a regular blender, blend soup in small batches and place a towel on blender top holding down firmly so the hot soup doesn't pop out of the blender and burn you. Taste and adjust seasoning if needed. Serve in bowls sprinkled with green onions.

*Vegan

DELICIOUSLY HOLISTIC

RAW CORN CHOWDER

Makes around 2–4 servings

This raw chowder is wonderful during the summer months when corn is extra sweet and juicy. The vanilla and smoked paprika add a smoky, warm, floral note that elevates the flavor of the corn. Corn provides the body with vitamin C, lutein, vitamin B1, vitamin E, magnesium, and fiber. Lutein is an important carotenoid that protects the eyes from macular degeneration.

4 cups organic corn kernels (5–6 ears)

2¼ cups unsweetened almond milk

1 clove peeled garlic—remove inner green stem

2 teaspoons fresh lemon juice

½ teaspoon smoked sweet paprika

⅛ teaspoon pure vanilla extract

½ avocado—peeled and seed removed

Unrefined sea salt and fresh black pepper to taste

For topping: blend together:

½ cup organic corn kernels

¼ cup diced organic red bell pepper

Remove husk and silk from corn and rinse well. Cut corn kernels off the cob with a sharp knife. Scrape cobs to remove corn milk. Reserve the cobs to make my recipe for corn stock. Reserve ½ cup of corn kernels to top soup with. In high-speed blender, puree together 3½ cups corn kernels with almond milk, garlic, lemon juice, smoked paprika, vanilla, avocado half, sea salt, and black pepper until smooth. Strain soup through a fine mesh strainer to have a smooth consistency. If you like the soup warm, place in saucepan and heat gently over low heat until warm. Taste and adjust seasoning. Place in bowl and top with corn kernels and bell pepper.

*Raw Vegan

DELICIOUSLY HOLISTIC

RAW WATERMELON JICAMA SOUP

Makes around 2–3 servings

This delicious cold soup features sweet watermelon, coconut water, and Jicama. It is full of vitamin C, electrolytes from the coconut water, fiber, and antioxidants which help fight free radicals. Watermelon is an excellent source of lycopene a carotenoid and important fat-soluble antioxidant which helps protect the body from free radicals. Jicama is a sweet and nutty tasting root vegetable that provides a crunchy, crisp, contrast to the refreshing soup and adds a high amount of vitamin C and potassium.

1 chilled small watermelon half—peeled, seeds removed, and cut into large chunks (use 3 cups)

½ cup young coconut water

½ cup diced Jicama

½ cup diced watermelon

1 teaspoon extra virgin olive oil

1 teaspoon raw honey—optional

1 teaspoon torn mint leaves—optional

Place all ingredients except diced Jicama, ½ cup diced watermelon, olive oil, honey, and mint into a high-speed blender and puree until smooth. Taste and add honey if needed. Toss Jicama and diced watermelon in olive oil until well mixed. Place small mounds of Jicama watermelon relish inside soup bowls and pour soup on top. Sprinkle with mint. If you want a smoother soup, strain it through a fine mesh strainer before placing in soup bowls.

*Raw Vegan

CHICKEN COCONUT SOUP

Makes around 4–6 servings

I love Asian cuisine, so I decided to create a chicken soup with a lovely lemongrass coconut broth which was inspired by the soups that I enjoy at Asian restaurants. This soup is full of bright flavors and essential nutrients, which come from all of the vegetables, chicken, coconut milk, and fresh herbs. To make a flavor-filled vegan version, leave out the chicken and use vegetable stock.

2 teaspoons garlic ginger paste*

1 cup organic unsweetened coconut milk—preservative free

7 cups organic chicken stock

3 organic carrots—peeled and sliced into ¼-inch rounds

1 (3-inch) piece of lemongrass—peeled and inner core grated on a Microplane

2 stalks organic celery—sliced into ¼-inch pieces

2 tablespoons organic Nama® Shoyu soy sauce or wheat-free Tamari

½ teaspoon cayenne pepper

3 cups chopped cooked skinless chicken breast meat

2 cups baby bok choy—sliced in small pieces (chiffonade)

½ cup sliced green onions

¼ cup chopped fresh Thai basil or cilantro

1 cup mung bean sprouts

1 fresh lemon—cut in half

Place all the ingredients except chicken, bok choy, green onion, basil or cilantro, mung beans, and lemon in a stockpot. Simmer over medium heat for 30 minutes or until vegetables are tender. Add chicken and bok choy during the last 15 minutes and cook until chicken is hot and bok choy is tender. Ladle soup into soup bowls and sprinkle each bowl with green onion, basil or cilantro, and mung beans. Squeeze fresh lemon juice to taste and serve immediately. ✑

***To make garlic-ginger paste:** Grate 2 garlic cloves and a 1-inch piece of ginger on Microplane and sprinkle with sea salt. Use back of knife to smash together until mixture becomes a paste.

SUMPTUOUS SALADS WITH IRRESISTIBLE VINAIGRETTES AND DRESSINGS

SUMPTUOUS SALADS MADE FROM A WIDE VARIETY OF SEASONAL, FRESH, COLORFUL PRODUCE AND IRRESISTIBLE HOMEMADE VINAIGRETTES AND DRESSINGS SHOULD BE AN INTEGRAL PART OF YOUR WEEKLY DIET. WHEN YOU EAT SALADS WHICH CONTAIN A WIDE VARIETY OF DIFFERENT COLORS, FLAVORS, TEXTURES, AND TASTES, YOU WILL NEVER GET BORED. SALADS MADE WITH THESE INGREDIENTS ARE DELECTABLE, VIBRANT, HEALTH-PROMOTING, AND FILLED WITH PHYTOCHEMICALS, VITAMINS, MINERALS, FIBER, ANTIOXIDANTS, CHLOROPHYLL, AND HEALTHY FATS. THESE SALADS WILL MAKE YOU FEEL SATISFIED AND WILL GIVE YOUR BODY WHAT IT NEEDS TO REPLENISH AND REJUVENATE.

TO MAKE YOUR SALAD PREPARATION QUICK AND EASY, TAKE 2–3 DAYS PER WEEK TO CHOP ALL THE FRESH VEGETABLES YOU WILL USE DURING THE WEEK. STORE THIS PRODUCE IN AIRTIGHT CONTAINERS AND USE TO TOP FRESH, LEAFY GREENS. I LIKE TO CHOP AND STORE CARROTS, RADISHES, ZUCCHINI, BABY BOK CHOY, BROCCOLI, CUCUMBERS, CELERY, RED CABBAGE, FENNEL, BELL PEPPERS, AND BEETS SO THAT I CAN COME UP WITH AN INFINITE NUMBER OF SALAD COMBINATIONS IN MINUTES. I ALSO LIKE TO MAKE SEVERAL DRESSINGS OR VINAIGRETTES AT THE BEGINNING OF THE WEEK SO I CAN TOSS TOGETHER ANY SALAD IN MINUTES WITH NO EXCUSES, SINCE EVERYTHING IS READY TO GO. AT THE END OF THE WEEK, IF I HAVE ANY LEFTOVERS, I ADD THEM INTO SMOOTHIES, LIQUID SALADS, SANDWICHES, SOUPS, SNACKS, OR VEGETABLE SIDE DISHES.

A GREAT, COLORFUL, NUTRIENT-RICH, AND FLAVOR-FILLED ADDITION IS EDIBLE FLOWERS. SOME GOOD EDIBLE FLOWER CHOICES INCLUDE NASTURTIUMS, PANSIES, HIBISCUS, BORAGE, BASIL, CHIVE, CHAMOMILE, APPLE BLOSSOMS, ZUCCHINI BLOSSOMS, FENNEL, AND ARUGULA FLOWERS. THE FOLLOWING RECIPES INCLUDE SOME OF MY FAVORITE SALADS AND DRESSINGS THAT I EAT ON A DAILY BASIS. AFTER TRYING THESE RECIPES, FEEL FREE TO USE YOUR CREATIVITY TO COME UP WITH YOUR OWN COMBINATIONS THAT ENGAGE YOUR SENSES AND EXCITE YOUR PALATE.

MEYER LEMON MISO DRESSING

Makes around 1 cup

White miso is a fermented soybean and rice paste filled with enzymes that has a delicate, salty flavor that blends well with the tangy lemon, sweet honey, Meyer lemon olive oil, and spicy ginger. This dressing is filled with vitamins, minerals, probiotics, and antioxidants and is wonderful on any leafy green salad.

2 tablespoons raw honey

2 teaspoons fresh peeled ginger—grated

1 organic Meyer lemon—peel, use flesh and juice from lemon

2 tablespoons white miso—non-genetically modified

⅓ cup O Meyer lemon extra virgin olive oil or your favorite extra virgin olive oil

1 teaspoon filtered water

In blender, blend all ingredients until smooth and creamy. Taste and adjust seasoning if needed. Store dressing in glass jar in the refrigerator for up to 1 week. ✎

*Raw Vegan

BLOOD ORANGE MAPLE DRESSING

Makes around ¾ cup

This dressing features blood oranges, which have a beautiful orange-red color and a flavor that is reminiscent of raspberries and oranges blended together. The blood orange juice adds a fresh citrus note, which I love. The maple syrup adds a wonderful sweetness to this dressing along with key minerals like manganese and zinc. Enjoy this dressing with all types of salads.

2 tablespoons organic maple syrup—grade B

2 teaspoons Dijon mustard

2 tablespoons raw apple cider vinegar

2 tablespoons fresh blood orange juice*

¼ teaspoon unrefined sea salt

Pinch fresh ground black pepper

½ cup O Blood orange extra virgin olive oil or your favorite extra virgin olive oil

Blend all ingredients except olive oil in small glass jar and whisk with fork until smooth. Add olive oil, screw on top, and shake until olive oil is blended in. Taste and add additional maple syrup if you like dressing sweeter. Store dressing in glass jar in the refrigerator for up to 1 week. ✎

*If you don't have the fresh blood orange juice, you can add your favorite orange juice.

AGED BALSAMIC VINAIGRETTE

Makes around ½ cup

AGED BALSAMIC VINEGAR is my favorite vinegar. It has an irresistible sweet, yet tangy flavor and wonderful consistency that is delicious drizzled on anything. O California balsamic vinegar and all of their wine vinegars are barrel aged in oak using the traditional Orleans method of aging without using any preservatives, chemicals, or mechanical methods. This process yields a complex, rich flavor that really elevates whatever foods you use them with. When you make this vinaigrette, be sure to use a top-quality cold pressed extra virgin olive oil like O Olive Oil or California Olive Ranch to enhance the flavor of the balsamic vinegar.

2 tablespoons O aged California balsamic or port balsamic vinegar

1 teaspoon Dijon mustard

Unrefined sea salt—to taste

5–6 tablespoons extra virgin olive oil

Blend all ingredients except olive oil in small glass jar and whisk until smooth. Add olive oil, screw on top, and shake until olive oil is blended in. Taste and adjust seasoning. Store dressing in glass jar in the refrigerator for up to 4 weeks.

*Raw Vegan

CLEMENTINE CASSIS DRESSING

Makes around ¾ cup

Cassis vinegar is fermented from black currants. Clementine oranges are seedless, sweet, thin-skinned Mandarin oranges from the tangerine family. These two flavors create a wonderful vinaigrette when paired together. If you can't find Clementine oranges, substitute a tangerine.

2 tablespoons O Cassis vinegar

1 teaspoon Dijon mustard

1 peeled Clementine orange or 1 peeled tangerine

6 tablespoons O Clementine extra virgin olive oil or your favorite extra virgin olive oil

½ teaspoon unrefined sea salt

Pinch fresh ground black pepper

Blend all ingredients in blender until smooth. Taste and adjust seasoning. Store dressing in glass jar in the refrigerator for up 5 days. ∽

CLEMENTINE CHAMPAGNE DRESSING

Follow directions for dressing but substitute champagne vinegar for the cassis vinegar and add 1 tablespoon of organic maple syrup with all the ingredients. Blend all ingredients in blender until smooth. Taste and adjust seasoning. Store dressing in glass jar in the refrigerator for up to 5 days. ∽

*Raw Vegan

CHERRY ALMOND DRESSING

Makes around 1 cup

SWEET DARK CHERRIES are delectable in this dressing. Pairing these cherries with almond butter makes a creamy, smooth dressing with healthy fat, fiber, and essential fatty acids from the almonds. Sweet cherries are full of flavonoids, quercetin, vitamin C, and fiber, which help protect the body against cancer and fight inflammation.

½ cup organic Bing cherries—pitted

3 tablespoons fresh orange juice

¼ cup sprouted or raw almond butter

Pinch unrefined sea salt

1 packet stevia or 1 teaspoon raw honey—optional

Blend all ingredients in a blender until smooth. Taste and add sweetener if needed. Dressing will stay fresh for 3–4 days covered in the refrigerator.

*Raw Vegan

MEYER LEMON CHAMPAGNE VINAIGRETTE

Makes around ¾ cup

MEYER LEMONS are less tart and less acidic than regular Eureka lemons, and they have a pronounced lemon flavor which is wonderful in this vinaigrette. Meyer lemons are available from December through April in local farmers' markets and are worth seeking out.

2 tablespoons fresh Meyer lemon juice*

2 tablespoons champagne vinegar

1 teaspoon Dijon mustard

½ cup O Meyer lemon extra virgin olive oil or your favorite extra virgin olive oil

Unrefined sea salt to taste

Fresh ground black pepper to taste

In glass jar with lid, whisk together lemon juice, champagne vinegar, and Dijon mustard. Add remaining ingredients, place lid on jar, and shake until dressing is combined.

*If you can't find Meyer lemons, substitute regular lemons and proceed with the recipe.

*Raw Vegan

MANGO GINGER DRESSING

Makes around 1½ cups

MANGO AND GINGER have a natural affinity for each other. Once you combine these ingredients with olive oil, orange juice, cayenne pepper, and honey, you have a sweet and spicy dressing that is irresistible and filled with antioxidants, enzymes, vitamins, and minerals. Use this dressing on shredded raw curly kale mixed with red cabbage for a great taste matchup.

1 cup fresh mango cubes

2 teaspoons fresh peeled ginger—grated

¼ cup extra virgin olive oil

2 tablespoons fresh orange juice

1 tablespoon champagne vinegar

¼ teaspoon unrefined sea salt

⅛ teaspoon cayenne pepper

1 teaspoon raw honey or ⅛ teaspoon or 1 packet stevia

Blend all dressing ingredients in a blender until smooth. Taste and adjust seasoning. Dressing will last for 2 days covered in the refrigerator. ➳

*Raw Vegan

HEIRLOOM TOMATO CREAM DRESSING

Makes around 2 cups

THIS DRESSING is wonderful when tomatoes are in their peak season. You can try any of the juicy and unique varieties of heirloom tomatoes available at your local farmers' markets. Adding the fat from the avocado to this dressing enables key phytonutrients from the tomatoes, like lycopene, to be absorbed better, and it also makes the dressing creamy.

2 large Heirloom or organic beefsteak tomatoes—remove stems and cut in half
3 oven-dried tomatoes (recipe on page 60)
1 large avocado—remove skin and seed
¼ cup fresh lemon juice
Unrefined sea salt to taste
Fresh ground Black pepper to taste

Place all ingredients in a high-speed blender and blend until smooth and creamy. Taste and adjust seasoning. Dressing will last covered in the refrigerator for 3–4 days.

*Raw Vegan

GOJI BERRY KOMBUCHA DRESSING

Makes ½ cup

KOMBUCHA TEA makes a wonderful, effervescent dressing that is full of health-promoting nutrients, enzymes, and probiotics to help your body rejuvenate. Feel free to use your favorite brand and flavor of Kombucha tea to create different salad dressing flavors.

2 tablespoons raw tahini
1 tablespoon raw honey
Pinch unrefined sea salt
¼ teaspoon cinnamon
3 tablespoons fresh orange juice
3 tablespoons goji berry Kombucha tea

In small glass jar with a lid, add all ingredients except Kombucha and stir to combine. Blend Kombucha in slowly and stir until smooth. Taste and add more orange juice if the dressing is too thick. Dressing will last for 5–7 days covered in the refrigerator.

*Raw Vegan

CARROT TAHINI DRESSING

Makes around 2½ cups

I created this dressing for the I Love Raw event in 2010 at Erewhon Natural Market in Los Angeles. Erewhon Natural Market is a pioneer and trendsetter in the health field and carries every type of health food product that you could possibly want. The dressing was a big hit, and I served it with lots of fresh cut-up organic vegetables from the farmers' market for dipping. This dressing uses raw tahini from Rejuvenative Foods, which is made from raw sesame seeds and can be found at many supermarkets.

¾ cup raw tahini

1 large peeled Navel orange

¼ cup spring or filtered water

¾ cup organic carrots—peeled and chopped

2 tablespoons O Blood orange extra virgin olive oil

2 teaspoons unrefined sea salt

1 stalk organic celery—chopped

2 cloves peeled garlic—grated

Place all ingredients in a high-speed blender and blend until smooth. Add additional water if dressing is too thick. Place in a glass jar with lid and store in the refrigerator. Dressing will last for 3–5 days covered in the refrigerator.

*Raw Vegan

BLOOD ORANGE, AMBROSIA APPLE, AND BABY SPINACH SALAD

Makes 2 servings

BLOOD ORANGES have a beautiful, deep orange-red color and sweet flavor that tastes like a cross between a raspberry and orange. Blood oranges are available from November through May, so seek them out at this time. Oranges contain vitamin C, potassium, and flavonoids that provide many health benefits to the body. Ambrosia apples are delectable apples that are sweet, crisp, and low in acid. Their crunchy texture and fabulous flavor pair beautifully with the blood orange and baby spinach.

2 blood oranges*

4 cups organic baby spinach—rinsed and dried

1 organic ambrosia apple—cored, cut in half, and cut into ½-inch cubes

1 small organic red bell pepper—seeds and stem removed, pepper sliced in ¼-inch slices

¼–⅓ cup blood orange maple dressing (recipe on page 142)

Cut off ends of each orange and remove peel and white pith. Slice each orange crosswise into 5 or 6 ¼-inch slices or cut into individual segments. Set aside. Place baby spinach, cubed apples, red bell pepper slices, and oranges in large bowl and toss with enough dressing to coat. Serve immediately on salad plates. ❧

*You can substitute any orange if blood oranges are not in season.

*Raw Vegan

CRANBERRY TUNA SALAD

Makes 2–4 servings

TUNA FISH SALAD is delicious on top of a leafy green salad. I created a mayo-free tuna salad which is good drizzled with many of the vinaigrettes or dressings in this book. Wild albacore or yellowfin tuna is a low mercury tuna that is caught by sustainable methods. I added dried cranberries to this tuna salad to give it a sweet and tart bite. The brands of tuna I love and recommend are Wild Planet or Crown Prince Natural.

2 (5 or 6-ounce) cans Wild Planet wild albacore or Crown Prince Natural wild yellowfin tuna in spring water

2 organic celery ribs—sliced finely

1 peeled small red onion—thinly sliced

1 large avocado—cut into medium chunks

2 tablespoons fresh lemon juice

½ cup dried unsulfured cranberries

Unrefined sea salt

Fresh ground black pepper

6 cups organic mixed baby greens—rinsed, dried, and chilled

Aged balsamic vinaigrette or dressing of choice

In medium-size mixing bowl, add drained tuna and flake into small pieces. Add celery slices, onion slices, chopped avocado, lemon juice, and dried cranberries and stir lightly to combine. Season the tuna salad to taste with small amount of sea salt and fresh ground black pepper. Sprinkle tuna salad on top of mixed greens and drizzle with vinaigrette or dressing. Serve immediately. ⌒

CHICKEN VEGETABLE QUINOA SALAD

Makes 3–4 servings

QUINOA is an ancient seed that originates from South America and is eaten like a grain. I can't get enough of the flavor and fluffy texture that pops in your mouth. Quinoa's nutritional profile is amazing and includes a high amount of protein, essential amino acids, vitamin B2, vitamin E, magnesium, manganese, calcium, iron, zinc, copper, omega-3, and fiber. Make sure you soak your quinoa overnight and rinse well before cooking to remove the anti-nutrients and saponin coating, which is bitter.

1 cup quinoa—soaked overnight in purified water with 2 tablespoons fresh lemon juice or raw apple cider vinegar added

2 cups filtered water

1 cup shredded roasted organic chicken

1 diced organic Persian cucumber

¾ cup micro greens—rinse well and pat dry

1 medium diced avocado

¼ cup sliced green onion

⅓–½ cup Meyer Lemon champagne vinaigrette (recipe on page 145)

Unrefined sea salt and fresh ground black pepper to taste

After soaking, rinse quinoa thoroughly and drain well. Place 2 cups of filtered water in saucepan and bring to a boil. Reduce the heat to medium, stir in the quinoa, cover, and cook for around 15 minutes. When quinoa is cooked, the grains will be slightly translucent and soft. Cool quinoa down to room temperature. Place quinoa and all salad ingredients in bowl and toss with ⅓ cup salad dressing. Taste and add more dressing if needed. Season the salad to taste with sea salt and fresh ground black pepper. ✑

VEGAN VERSION

Omit chicken, add 1 cup of your favorite seasonal chopped vegetables, and follow the recipe. ✑

ARUGULA COMICE PEAR SALAD

Makes 2 servings

COMICE PEARS are a truly delicious, juicy pear with a sweet, delicate flavor and wonderful texture that pairs nicely with the peppery arugula and crunchy pumpkin seeds. Comice pears are available from September to March, so look for them in your local farmers' markets or natural food stores. If you can't find these pears, then substitute your favorite pear to make this recipe. Pears are high in pectin, which is a water-soluble fiber that can help lower cholesterol. Pears are also a good source of potassium, vitamin B2, and vitamin C. The pumpkin seeds add great texture and flavor along with omega-3 fatty acids, zinc, and iron.

2 firm organic Comice pears—remove cores, cut in half

1 teaspoon fresh lemon juice

2 cups organic wild or wasabi arugula—rinsed and dried

4 cups organic mixed baby greens—rinsed and dried

⅓ cup blood orange maple dressing (recipe on page 142)

½ cup sprouted or raw pumpkin seeds

Thinly slice pear halves on Mandoline. Toss cut pear slices in lemon juice. Toss arugula, baby greens, and pears with enough dressing to evenly coat salad. Place on serving plates and sprinkle with the pumpkin seeds. ⌒

*Raw Vegan

WATERMELON RADISH, GOLDEN BEET, AND WATERCRESS SALAD

Serves 2–4

WATERMELON or beauty heart radishes are a root vegetable which has a vivid pink and white inside and green outside that looks like a watermelon when sliced. You can usually find these gorgeous radishes at your local farmers' market. Radishes are a great beauty food that is a rich source of vitamin C and sulfur which is important for building and maintaining collagen. Watercress is a favorite of mine and is a potent blood builder with anti-cancer properties. The watermelon radish pairs perfectly with the red onions, golden beets, cherries, lemon miso dressing, peppery watercress, baby greens, and crunchy sweet pecans. If you can't find the watermelon radishes, substitute red globe radishes.

3 watermelon or red globe radishes—cut in ⅛-inch-thick slices

3 cups organic watercress greens—rinsed and dried

3 cups organic mixed baby greens—rinsed and dried

½ small red onion—peeled and thinly sliced

1 golden beet—peeled and grated

⅓ cup Living Nutz celestial cina-pecans or raw pecans—chopped

⅓ cup unsulfured dried cherries

⅓–½ cup Meyer lemon miso dressing (recipe on page 142)

In a large bowl, toss together radish slices, watercress, baby greens, red onion, grated beet, pecans, and cherries. Toss with enough dressing to coat and place on salad plates. Serve immediately.

*Raw Vegan

RAW BEET TARTARE

Makes 3–4 servings

BEETS are a versatile root vegetable that I adore. Both the root and greens or leaves are edible. Beets are sweet and come in a variety of colors. Raw beets are a potent blood purifier and liver detoxifier. Beets also contain betacyanin, which helps protect the body against cancer. The beets and the beet greens are a good source of iron, potassium, B vitamins, vitamin A, vitamin C, and calcium. This raw beet tartare is sweet, crunchy, and slightly spicy, and the beet greens add a good level of nutrients and a delicate, refreshing flavor that is a nice contrast to the beets.

1 large red beet—peeled and cut in large cubes

⅛–¼ teaspoon cayenne pepper (depending on how spicy you like the tartare)

1 tablespoon fresh parsley leaves

1 cup thinly shredded beet greens or micro greens—rinsed and dried

⅓ cup plus 3 tablespoons clementine champagne dressing (recipe on page 144)

Unrefined sea salt to taste

Blend all ingredients except beet greens and 1 tablespoon of the dressing in food processor and process until it resembles large rice grains. Season the tartare to taste with sea salt. Press half of mixture into 3.5-inch ring mold placed on top of salad plate. Press down firmly with a large spoon. Toss beet greens or micro greens with 1 tablespoon of vinaigrette and sea salt to taste and carefully top each tartare with an equal amount of greens. Carefully remove ring molds. Repeat with other plates and remaining beet mixture and greens. Serve immediately. ❧

*Raw Vegan

RED CABBAGE APPLE SALAD

Serves 2–3

RED CABBAGE is a member of the cruciferous family, which also includes many other vegetables like collard greens, kale, broccoli, mustard greens, bok choy, and cauliflower. Cabbage is a superfood vegetable that is a potent cancer fighter due to the presence of glucosinolates. Cabbage is rich in vitamin C, vitamin B6, calcium, potassium, magnesium, and biotin. I love the flavor of red cabbage and enjoy eating it cooked or raw. This salad is delicious on its own or served as a side dish.

3 cups red cabbage—cut into fine strips by hand or shredded in the food processor

1 cup shredded organic carrots

1 large organic apple—cored, cut in half, and sliced in ¼-inch slices or 1-inch cubes

¼–⅓ cup clementine cassis dressing (recipe on page 144)

Unrefined sea salt to taste

Combine all salad ingredients except dressing in large bowl and toss with ¼ cup of dressing to coat vegetables and apples. Add additional dressing if needed. Season the salad to taste with sea salt and chill for 30 minutes to let flavors meld.

*Raw Vegan

BUTTERNUT SQUASH MIXED BABY GREENS SALAD

Serves 2–4

BUTTERNUT SQUASH is wonderful roasted because it becomes caramelized and buttery. Butternut squash is rich in carotenes, fiber, and vitamin C. I really like this salad because it combines the sweet from the squash, salty from the Parmigiano, and crunchy from the walnuts into one wonderful salad. Parmigiano Reggiano is an aged raw milk cheese from Italy which has great flavor and healthy probiotics and enzymes. You can use parmesan cheese if you can't get the Parmigiano Reggiano.

1 small butternut squash—peeled, seeded, and cut into 1-inch cubes (3 cups)

2 tablespoons melted organic unsalted clarified butter or virgin coconut oil

2 tablespoons organic maple syrup—grade B

¼ teaspoon unrefined sea salt

Freshly ground black pepper

6 cups organic mixed baby greens—rinsed and dried

½ cup aged balsamic vinaigrette (recipe on page 143)

¼ cup Parmigiano Reggiano—shaved with vegetable peeler

⅓ cup Living Nutz passionate pesto walnuts or raw walnuts

Preheat oven to 400° F. Toss butternut squash with melted clarified butter or coconut oil, maple syrup, and sprinkle with sea salt and black pepper. Line a baking sheet with parchment paper or a silicon mat, place squash on top, and roast for around 20 minutes until squash begins to brown. Turn squash over and continue to cook for an additional 15–20 minutes or until squash is golden brown and tender. Remove from oven and cool down slightly. Place baby greens in a bowl and top with roasted squash. Toss with enough balsamic vinaigrette to coat salad. Place on individual salad plates and top with shaved slices of Parmigiano Reggiano cheese, parmesan, or grated Daiya cheese and walnuts.

ITALIAN VEGETABLE SALAD WITH BLACK PEPPER CROUTONS

Serves 2–4

THIS ITALIAN SALAD contains a variety of vibrant colors and essential nutrients that come from all the different ingredients. The black pepper croutons add a crunchy, spicy element that pairs wonderfully with the baby romaine, tomatoes, and bell peppers. Feel free to add whatever combination of fresh seasonal vegetables you have on hand to create your ultimate salad.

3 slices sprouted or sourdough whole grain or gluten-free bread

2 tablespoons avocado oil or melted organic unsalted clarified butter

Fresh ground black pepper to taste

6 cups organic baby romaine—rinsed and dried

1 organic red bell pepper—finely chopped

1 small zucchini—shredded

½ cup oven-dried tomatoes (recipe on page 60)

½ small red onion—peeled and thinly sliced

1 English cucumber—thinly sliced

⅓ cup fresh basil leaves—torn into bite-size pieces

½ cup aged balsamic vinaigrette or heirloom tomato cream dressing

⅓ cup Gone Nuts sun-dried marinara almonds and pistachios—optional

Preheat oven to 400° F. Remove crust from bread slices, tear bread into large cubes, and place on greased baking pan. Drizzle bread lightly with avocado oil or melted butter and sprinkle with fresh ground black pepper. Toss bread cubes to coat well. Place bread in the oven. Bake until croutons are light brown and crispy, around 5 minutes. Be careful not to overcook the croutons. Set croutons aside while you make the salad.

Mix romaine greens, all the vegetables, and basil in a large bowl. Toss with enough dressing to lightly coat salad. Put salad on serving plates and top with black pepper croutons and the nuts if using.

*Vegan

HERB HEMP SEED SALAD

Makes around 5 cups

THIS SALAD is my take on a tabouli salad without the gluten from the bulgur wheat. The hemp seeds add protein, great texture, and nice crunch, which are wonderful in this salad. Hemp seeds have all the essential amino acids and are full of fiber. Hemp seeds have the perfect balance of omega-3 and 6 essential fatty acids. You can also add 2 cups of cooked, cooled quinoa for another flavorful variation.

2 cups minced flat-leaf parsley

¼ cup minced mint leaves

2 tablespoons green onions or scallions

¾ cup diced roma tomatoes

½ cup hemp seeds

1 cup diced organic Persian cucumber

½ cup diced pineapple

⅓ cup fresh lemon juice

¼ cup extra virgin olive oil

2 teaspoons unrefined sea salt

⅛ teaspoon fresh ground black pepper

In medium-size mixing bowl, blend all ingredients together. Taste and adjust seasoning. Cover and refrigerate until well chilled. Salad will last covered in the refrigerator for 2–3 days.

*Raw Vegan

DELICIOUSLY HOLISTIC

FUJI APPLE SALAD

Serves 2

I love to eat different varieties of apples from the farmers' market throughout the year. One of my favorite ways to enjoy them is made into a salad with creamy yogurt and topped with my favorite blend of nuts, seeds, and dried fruit. This salad makes a filling and satisfying snack and is also great for a quick breakfast. Apples are an excellent source of quercetin, which is a wonderful antioxidant that is a potent cancer fighter. Quercetin is located in the skin of apples, so always enjoy your apples with the skin on and buy them organic to avoid pesticides and waxes found on conventional apples.

1 large or 2 small organic Fuji apples—rinsed well and cut into small cubes

⅓ cup organic plain Greek yogurt or orange coconut yogurt (recipe on page 103)

1 teaspoon cinnamon

1 teaspoon pure vanilla extract

1 tablespoon raw honey, 2 tablespoons coconut sugar, or ¼ teaspoon or 2 packets stevia

½ cup of your favorite sprouted or raw trail mix

In medium-size bowl, place cut apples, yogurt, cinnamon, vanilla, and sweetener of choice. Mix well with a spoon and taste for sweetness. Add additional sweetener if needed. Place in serving dishes and sprinkle with your favorite mix of nuts, seeds, and dried fruit. If you have leftover salad, add a teaspoon of fresh lemon juice to keep the fruit from turning brown and place covered in the refrigerator for up to 1 day.

*Raw Vegan if made with coconut yogurt

YUZU CUCUMBER SALAD

Makes around 2 cups

PERSIAN CUCUMBERS are my favorite cucumber because they are sweet, juicy, and crunchy, with thin edible skins. Cucumbers are extremely hydrating because of their high water content. They are also high in vitamin C, vitamin A, folic acid, and fiber. The skin contains silica which maintains the strength of our body's connective tissue. Yuzu is a citron fruit from Japan with a distinct citrus flavor that tastes like a cross between a lemon, orange, and lime. Pairing the Yuzu vinegar with the cucumbers creates a refreshing, tangy salad that is perfect on a hot summer day.

4 organic Persian cucumbers—washed and dried

1 teaspoon unrefined sea salt

1 teaspoon coconut sugar or Rapadura

⅛ teaspoon fresh ground black pepper

⅓ cup O Yuzu vinegar*

Thinly slice cucumbers with a knife or Mandoline. Place in colander, sprinkle lightly with sea salt, and let cucumbers drain in sink for 15 minutes. Place drained cucumbers in bowl, sprinkle with coconut sugar or Rapadura and black pepper, and toss with the Yuzu vinegar. Cover and refrigerate for at least 20 minutes to allow flavors to meld.

*You can substitute raw apple cider vinegar for the Yuzu vinegar.

*Raw Vegan

SENSATIONAL SANDWICHES, WRAPS, AND ROLLS

I HAVE ALWAYS ENJOYED SANDWICHES, WRAPS, AND ROLLS. THEY ARE GREAT TO EAT FOR LUNCH OR AS PART OF AN EASY DINNER. THE FOLLOWING RECIPES USE SPROUTED GRAIN BREADS, LEAFY GREENS, AND NORI SEAWEED FOR THE OUTER PORTION OF THE SANDWICHES, WRAPS, AND ROLLS. WHOLE GRAINS CONTAIN ENZYME INHIBITORS AND PHYTATES THAT BIND MINERALS LIKE ZINC, IRON, CALCIUM, COPPER, AND MAGNESIUM. SOAKING IN ACIDIC WATER, SPROUTING, OR FERMENTING THE GRAINS REMOVES THE TANNINS, PHYTATES, AND ENZYMES INHIBITORS AND MAKES THE PROTEIN, VITAMINS, AND MINERALS AVAILABLE FOR YOUR BODY TO ABSORB. THIS MAKES THE GRAIN MORE NUTRITIOUS AND EASIER TO DIGEST. YOU CAN ALSO SUBSTITUTE WHEAT-FREE OR GLUTEN-FREE BREADS MADE WITH GLUTEN- AND WHEAT-FREE GRAINS IF YOU HAVE GLUTEN INTOLERANCE.

I ALSO LIKE TO USE LEAFY GREENS LIKE BUTTER LETTUCE OR ROMAINE AND RAW VEGAN BREADS BY COMPANIES LIKE THE RAW BAKERY, LYDIA'S ORGANICS, OR MAUK FAMILY FARMS. SOME OF THE SPROUTED GRAIN OR NATURALLY FERMENTED BREADS I RECOMMEND ARE BY GRINDSTONE BAKERY, ALVARADO STREET BAKERY, FOOD FOR LIFE, AND MANNA ORGANICS. ALL OF THESE COMPANIES USE ORGANIC WHOLE GRAINS AND ARE FREE OF CORN SYRUP. THESE COMPANIES ALSO MAKE VARIETIES OF BREAD, BUNS, BAGELS, AND ROLLS THAT ARE GLUTEN-FREE, WHEAT-FREE, PRESERVATIVE-FREE, AND YEAST-FREE. FEEL FREE TO CHOOSE THE BREAD AND COMPANY FROM THESE CHOICES WHICH MEETS YOUR NEEDS, BUDGET, AND TASTE.

WILD SALMON VEGETABLE SUSHI ROLLS

Makes 8 half rolls

WILD SALMON is a good source of essential omega-3 fatty acids and protein, which our bodies require on a daily basis. The combination of the wild salmon with the vegetables and avocado make a flavor-filled sushi roll without the addition of white rice.

YUZU SOY SAUCE

¼ cup organic Nama® Shoyu soy sauce or Tamari—wheat free

1 Tablespoon O Yuzu rice vinegar or regular rice wine vinegar

SUSHI ROLLS

2 small Avocados—cut in half and seed removed

1 teaspoon fresh grated wasabi or wasabi paste

2 teaspoons fresh peeled ginger—grated

4 sheets nori seaweed

1 cup wild Alaskan skinless, boneless canned salmon—flaked into pieces

1 organic Persian cucumber—julienned

1 organic carrot—julienned

2 green onions—use only the green part, sliced in long, thin strips

In small bowl blend together Nama® Shoyu or Tamari and Yuzu vinegar and set aside while you make the sushi rolls. In another small bowl, blend together avocado, wasabi, and ginger until smooth. Taste and add additional wasabi if you like it hotter. Place the nori sheet shiny side down on a sushi mat or cutting board in front of you. Spread ¼ cup of avocado mixture on top of the nori sheet on the side closest to you. Lay ¼ cup of salmon pieces, cucumber pieces, carrot pieces, and green onions on top of the avocado mixture. Moisten a 1" inch line on end of the nori sheet with water and carefully roll the nori around the salmon and vegetables, pulling the roll toward you as you roll it to make it tight. Slice the roll down the middle and slice each half in 4 pieces with a wet, sharp knife. Repeat with remaining nori sheets. Serve with Yuzu soy sauce. ✎

SARDINE LETTUCE WRAPS

Serves 2

SARDINES are an inexpensive, sustainable fish that is a good source of heart-healthy omega-3 fatty acids and protein. Most people consume way too many omega-6 fatty acids, which can lead to imbalances in the body. Eating sardines on a regular basis will help balance excess omega-6. Leaving in the delicate bones will provide a good amount of calcium.

2 cans sardines in olive oil or water—Wild Planet or Crown Prince is a good choice

1 tablespoon fresh lemon juice

½ teaspoon lemon zest

2 tablespoons organic plain Greek yogurt

Unrefined sea salt to taste

Fresh ground black pepper to taste

2–3 dashes hot pepper sauce

6 butter lettuce leaves—wash and pat dry

¼ cup cultured tomato pineapple salsa (recipe on page 65)

2 green onions—thinly sliced

Drain sardines and place in a small bowl. Mash sardines well, add remaining ingredients except lettuce leaves, salsa, and onion slices, and stir until well combined. Place sardines in lettuce leaves and top with salsa and green onions. ✑

MIXED VEGETABLE PEA SHOOTS SANDWICH

Serves 2

THIS SANDWICH is a great way to get in a large serving of nutrient-rich vegetables in one fantastic sandwich. Really try to find the pea shoots because they add a wonderful sweetness that pairs well with the vegetables and tomato.

4 slices sprouted whole grain bread or sourdough bread—toasted

Dijon mustard

2 cups any combination of seasonal vegetables like sliced cucumber, sliced red onions, sliced sweet bell pepper, sliced mushrooms, sliced radishes, and sliced zucchini

1 cup pea shoots

1 large heirloom or beefsteak tomato—sliced

1 large avocado—sliced and sprinkled with unrefined sea salt and ground black pepper

Homemade salad dressing or vinaigrette

Spread bread slices with Dijon mustard. Place vegetable choices, pea greens, tomato, and avocado between bread slices and drizzle with dressing or vinaigrette. Cut sandwiches in half and serve.

TIP FOR SLICING AVOCADO

Cut avocado in half. Using chef's knife blade, stick knife blade in center of seed, twist seed and remove. Use large spoon to scoop avocado half from shell. Place on cutting board and slice in ¼-inch-thick slices. Use immediately or avocado will turn brown. You can also squeeze lemon or lime juice on cut avocado to keep it from turning brown.

---

*Vegan

RAW ROMAINE TACOS

Serves 2–3

THIS PLAY ON A TACO is a great raw vegan alternative to a traditional taco. Its flavor is fresh, crispy, sweet, spicy, and creamy. This taco will fill your body with top nutrients and fiber along with enzymes from the peaches and tomatoes. You can also use my cultured tomato pineapple salsa in place of the salsa recipe listed here for a probiotic-rich alternative.

TOMATO PEACH SALSA

1½ cups diced heirloom or roma tomatoes

¾ cup peeled pitted peaches—cut in ¼-inch cubes

¼ cup organic cilantro leaves

⅓ cup sliced green onions

½ diced jalapeño pepper—seeds and stem removed

1 peeled garlic clove—grated

3 teaspoons fresh lemon juice

1 tsp unrefined sea salt

1 cup pumpkin seed spread (recipe on page 210)

8 large organic romaine heart leaves—rinsed and patted dry

Combine all ingredients in a mixing bowl except pumpkin seed spread and romaine leaves. Mix together until well combined. Set salsa aside while you assemble the tacos.

Assembly:

Line up romaine leaves on 2 plates. Spread ⅛ cup of pumpkin seed spread on each leaf. Top each romaine leaf with salsa and serve immediately. ᴄ

*Raw Vegan

PORTOBELLO MUSHROOM AND GRILLED ONION BURGERS

Serves 2

Portobello mushrooms have a sensational taste and meaty texture that is a great vegan option for meat eaters. The marinade in this recipe is smoky, spicy, tangy, and sweet. I serve these Portobello mushrooms like a traditional hamburger and top with baby romaine greens for an added kick of flavor and nutrients.

MARINADE

2 tablespoons Balsamic vinegar

⅓ cup extra virgin olive oil or avocado oil

1 tablespoon wheat-free Tamari or organic Nama® Shoyu soy sauce

⅛ teaspoon smoked sweet paprika

1 peeled garlic clove—grated or minced

⅛ teaspoon cayenne pepper

2 teaspoons organic maple syrup—grade B

BURGERS

4 large Portobello mushrooms—cleaned and patted dry

1 large white onion—peeled and cut into thick slices

Olive oil or avocado oil to cook mushrooms and onions in

2 sprouted whole grain hamburger buns—toasted

Dijon mustard

¼ cup baby romaine lettuce—washed and patted dry

In small bowl mix together all ingredients for the marinade. Scrape dark gills from mushroom caps using a spoon. Place cleaned mushrooms and sliced onions in the marinade and coat completely. Let mushrooms and onions marinate for 30 minutes. Place large skillet or grill pan on medium heat and drizzle with oil. Add marinated mushrooms and onions to hot pan and cook until onions and mushrooms are soft, around 10–15 minutes. Turn over mushrooms and onions halfway through the cooking time. Place two mushrooms on each of the toasted buns spread with Dijon mustard; top with onions and romaine and serve immediately. ꔷ

*Vegan

DELECTABLE DINNER ENTRÉES

THIS SECTION IS CALLED "DELECTABLE DINNER ENTRÉES" BECAUSE THEY ARE MADE WITH WILD SEAFOOD, ORGANIC OR PASTURE-RAISED LAND ANIMALS, AND ORGANIC VEGETABLES THAT REALLY MAKE A DIFFERENCE IN THE QUALITY, NUTRITIONAL VALUE, AND TASTE OF THE RECIPES. I HAVE INCLUDED A VARIETY OF RECIPES THAT USE WILD, SUSTAINABLE SEAFOOD, PASTURE-RAISED OR ORGANIC CHICKEN, ORGANIC, PASTURE-RAISED, GRASS-FED BEEF, PASTURE-RAISED LAMB, AND PLANT-BASED ENTRÉES FOR PEOPLE WHO PREFER TO EAT THIS WAY.

IF YOU EAT ANIMAL-BASED PROTEIN, IT IS ESSENTIAL TO YOUR HEALTH AND THE HEALTH OF OUR PLANET TO CHOOSE SUSTAINABLE WILD SEAFOOD, ORGANIC MEATS, AND POULTRY THAT ARE PASTURE-RAISED, HUMANELY TREATED, AND FED A NATURAL DIET WITHOUT ANY ANTIBIOTICS, HORMONES, STEROIDS, AND ANIMAL BY-PRODUCTS. ORGANIC PASTURE-RAISED ANIMALS PROVIDE ESSENTIAL OMEGA-3 FATTY ACIDS, BETA-CAROTENE, VITAMINS B12, VITAMIN E, CLA, KEY MINERALS, AND PROTEIN. ORGANIC PASTURE-RAISED ANIMALS' DIETS AND LIFESTYLES PRODUCE MEATS AND POULTRY THAT ARE LEANER AND HEALTHIER THAN FACTORY-FARM-RAISED ANIMALS.

WILD SEAFOOD IS A SUSTAINABLE SEAFOOD CHOICE THAT IS NUTRIENT-RICH AND A WONDERFUL SOURCE OF PROTEIN AND ESSENTIAL OMEGA-3 FATTY ACIDS. IF YOU ENJOY EATING MEAT, POULTRY, OR SEAFOOD, TRY TO CUT BACK EATING IT TO 4–5 DAYS PER WEEK AND EAT VEGAN FOR THE OTHER 2–3 DAYS. EATING LIKE THIS GIVES YOU THE BEST OF BOTH WORLDS, INCREASES YOUR INTAKE OF PLANT FOODS, AND WILL SAVE MONEY ON YOUR MONTHLY FOOD BILL AND ALLOW YOU TO SPLURGE ON THE MORE EXPENSIVE ORGANIC, PASTURE-RAISED MEATS, POULTRY AND WILD SEAFOOD.

WILD ALASKAN SALMON PATTIES

Makes 6–8 patties

WILD ALASKAN SALMON is one of the healthiest cold-water fish you can eat. It provides your body with heart-healthy omega-3 fatty acids, quality protein, vitamin B12, potassium, and selenium. Wild Salmon also helps protect the body against heart disease and many types of cancer. Wild salmon is one of the top sources of omega-3 essential fatty acids. Eating salmon on a regular basis will help you enjoy the benefits of omega-3 for cardiovascular and immune system health. This recipe uses inexpensive canned salmon, which is good to use for this patty. Bumble Bee has a good red sockeye salmon in a 14.75-ounce size, so if you choose this brand, use 1 can in the recipe and reduce the amount of sea salt used.

2 (7.5-ounce) cans wild sockeye salmon—drained, bones and skin removed (save liquid)

⅓ cup peeled shallots—finely chopped

⅓ cup organic orange bell pepper—finely chopped, seeds and ribs removed

⅓ cup organic celery—finely chopped

¼ teaspoon unrefined sea salt

¼ teaspoon fresh ground black pepper

½ teaspoon onion powder

½ teaspoon garlic powder

1 teaspoon fresh lemon juice

1 large egg

¼ cup organic unsalted clarified butter or virgin coconut oil

Drain juice from salmon cans into a cup and reserve for later. Remove bones and skin from salmon and place in mixing bowl. Flake salmon and add shallots, bell pepper, celery, sea salt, black pepper, onion powder, garlic powder, and lemon juice. Add small amount of the reserved salmon juice to hold mixture together. Taste and adjust seasoning. Stir in egg. Refrigerate for ½ hour. Remove from refrigerator and form into small, round patties. Place on plate. Heat clarified butter or coconut oil in a large skillet on medium heat until hot but not smoking. Pan fry the salmon patties until golden brown on both sides, about 3–5 minutes per side. Drain on paper towels and serve immediately. ❧

LEMON HERB WILD BLACK COD

Makes 4 servings

WILD BLACK COD is a sustainable wild fish with a wonderful flavor and rich white flesh. Black cod or sablefish is a great source of protein, essential omega-3 fatty acids, and selenium. Black cod contains more omega-3 essential fatty acids than wild salmon. Vital Choice Wild Seafood has wonderful black cod fillets and they deliver directly to your home. You can also substitute wild Pacific cod from Alaska. The lemon and fresh herbs really complement the rich taste of the black cod.

4 (4-ounce) skinless, boneless wild black cod (sablefish) fillets—1-inch thick

3 tablespoons finely chopped fresh chives

1 teaspoon finely chopped fresh lemon thyme leaves

2 teaspoons finely chopped fresh parsley leaves

2 tablespoons finely chopped fresh basil leaves

½ teaspoon lemon zest

2 cloves peeled garlic—grated

2 tablespoons fresh lemon juice

2 tablespoons melted organic unsalted clarified butter or avocado oil

Unrefined sea salt and fresh ground black pepper to taste

Preheat oven to 375° F. Check for any large pin bones and remove from black cod with a pair of fish pliers or tweezers. Place parchment paper in bottom of 9x13-inch baking dish. Mix together chives, thyme, parsley, basil, lemon zest, and garlic on top of parchment paper in baking dish and spread across the bottom of pan. In small bowl mix together lemon juice and melted butter or avocado oil, and coat fillets on both sides in oil and then in herb mixture. Sprinkle fish with sea salt and black pepper to taste. Bake fish uncovered in oven for around 8–9 minutes or until fish feels slightly firm to the touch and is opaque in the center. Check doneness by inserting a knife in the center of the fish and checking the color. Serve immediately.

LEMONGRASS GINGER WILD SALMON

Makes 4 servings

The ginger, garlic, lemongrass, tamari, and maple syrup create a citrusy, delicious, Asian inspired marinade that really complements the wild Alaskan salmon. Wild salmon provides your body with heart healthy omega-3 essential fatty acids, quality protein, vitamin B12, potassium, and selenium. Since your body can't make essential fatty acids they must come from the foods you eat. Eating salmon on a regular basis will help you enjoy the benefits of omega-3 for cardiovascular and immune system health. Sockeye salmon is also an excellent source of vitamin D and astaxanthin a carotene and potent antioxidant. Slow roasting the salmon at a low temperature creates a wonderful silky texture and keeps the fish from overcooking. If you can't find lemongrass, omit from the recipe and add 1 teaspoon of grated fresh lemon zest instead.

4 (6-ounce) wild Sockeye or Coho salmon fillets (1¼-inches thick)

¼ cup plus 2 teaspoons organic Nama® Shoyu soy sauce or Tamari

¼ cup organic maple syrup—grade B

1 teaspoon peeled ginger—grated

¼ teaspoon peeled garlic cloves—grated

1 teaspoon peeled lemongrass—grated

1 teaspoon extra virgin olive oil

1 tablespoon minced fresh green onions—reserve to use as a garnish

Check for any large pin bones and remove from salmon with a pair of fish pliers or tweezers. Mix all ingredients except fish and green onions in a small bowl, whisking with a fork until well combined. Place fish fillets in a baking dish lined with parchment or lightly coated in oil and spread the marinade evenly over the fish. Marinate the fish in the refrigerator for 20 minutes. Remove fish from refrigerator and let sit at room temperature while oven is heating. Preheat the oven to 250° F. Bake the salmon for about 25–30 minutes. Check doneness by inserting a knife in the center of the fish. Knife should slide out easily when fish is done. Sprinkle with green onions and serve immediately. ☙

TIP FOR USING FRESH LEMONGRASS

Remove 1-inch off the bottom of the lemongrass root and cut off the reedy top. Peel off the first 2–3 outer layers of the lemongrass leaves until you get to the soft inner core. Now you can grate, slice, or dice the lemongrass and use in recipes. Lemongrass freezes well and will last for months in an airtight container or bag in the freezer.

3-HERB PESTO WILD HALIBUT

Serves 4

My 3-herb pesto is a nut-and-cheese-free blend of sweet basil, cilantro, and flat-leaf parsley, which adds a wonderful herb flavor which enhances the delicate wild halibut. The roasted cherry tomatoes on the vine are a great match and add additional nutrients like lycopene. Pacific wild halibut is a wonderful fish with a clean mild flavor and beautiful white color that is extremely versatile. Halibut is protein-rich and contains vitamin B12, potassium, omega-3 essential fatty acids, and selenium. My favorite way to enjoy halibut is with lots of fresh herbs and lemon and either pan roasted or oven roasted quickly to lock in the flavor and moisture. Halibut can easily overcook, so watch it carefully.

20 vine-ripe cherry tomatoes

4 tablespoons melted organic unsalted clarified butter or extra virgin olive oil

Unrefined sea salt to taste

Fresh ground pepper to taste

4 (6-ounce) skinless, boneless wild Pacific Halibut fillets (1-inch thick)

1 recipe for 3-Herb Pesto (recipe on page 62)

1 lemon—cut in half

Preheat oven to 350° F. Check for any large pin bones and remove from halibut with a pair of fish pliers or tweezers. Place parchment paper on a small baking sheet and place cherry tomatoes on it. Drizzle tomatoes with 2 tablespoons of clarified butter or olive oil and lightly sprinkle tomatoes with sea salt and black pepper. Place tomatoes in the oven and bake for around 30 minutes. When the tomatoes are done, turn off oven and leave inside to keep warm while you make the halibut. Sprinkle sea salt and pepper on top of halibut fillets. Heat a large skillet over medium-high heat for a few minutes until hot. Add 2 tablespoons of clarified butter in pan and heat until hot but not smoking. Place halibut fillets in hot pan and cook for around 4–5 minutes until golden brown in color. Turn over fillets, spread with generous amounts of 3-herb pesto, and continue to cook for 4–5 minutes or until fish is opaque in center only. Check doneness by inserting a knife in the center of the fish and checking the color. Squeeze fresh lemon juice on fillets while in pan and serve immediately. ✎

LIME MISO CORNISH GAME HENS

Serves 4

Miso is an Asian fermented paste made with soybeans, chickpeas, barley, or rice with a mild, salty flavor that pairs nicely with the lime, honey, and garlic. The enzyme-rich white miso has a milder flavor than some versions of miso, and it enhances rather than overpowers the game hen's delicate flavor. Fermenting the soybeans or chickpeas breaks down the enzyme inhibitors and phytates present in the soybeans or chickpeas and makes them easier to digest. Purchase organic miso only and avoid miso made with genetically modified soybeans. Eden Foods, South River Miso, or Miso Master® is a good choice.

3 tablespoons organic white miso paste

2 small limes—peel limes, leave whole, and remove all the white pith

2 tablespoons raw honey

5 tablespoons roasted garlic olive oil or your favorite extra virgin olive oil

2 large cloves peeled garlic—grated

¾ teaspoon unrefined sea salt

⅛ teaspoon fresh ground black pepper

2 large Cornish game hens—cleaned and cut in half

Sweet paprika

Blend together miso paste, peeled limes, raw honey, olive oil, garlic, sea salt, and black pepper in blender until smooth. Spread marinade all over game hen halves. Let hens marinate covered in the refrigerator for at least 2 hours or overnight. Remove marinated hens and place on lightly greased baking pan, sprinkle lightly with paprika, and let sit for 10 minutes at room temperature while oven preheats. Preheat oven to 375° F. Place Cornish hens in baking pan, pour 3 tablespoons of filtered water in bottom of pan, cover pan with foil, and bake for 30 minutes. Uncover pan and baste hens with pan juices. Continue cooking for an additional 30–45 minutes or until hens reach an internal temperature of 165° F. Baste occasionally during cooking with pan juices. Remove hens, cover, and let rest for 10 minutes. Carryover cooking once the hens are removed from oven should raise the internal temperature of hens an additional 5°–10° F higher.

DIJON HONEY CHICKEN WINGS

Serves 2–3

These baked chicken wings are a tasty alternative to deep-fat-fried chicken wings. The Dijon mustard and lemon, along with the other ingredients, forms a tangy, rich coating for the chicken wings, which makes them tender, juicy, and full of flavor. Chicken contains protein, B vitamins, and selenium.

⅓ cup Dijon mustard

½ medium peeled lemon—remove all the white pith

¼ cup raw honey

1 teaspoon unrefined sea salt

2 large cloves peeled garlic—grated

⅛ teaspoon fresh ground black pepper

12 whole chicken wings—rinsed and patted dry

½ teaspoon Paprika

Preheat oven to 400° F. Blend together all ingredients in a blender except chicken wings and paprika until smooth. Taste and add more sea salt or black pepper to taste. Set aside for later. Remove tips from cleaned wings and cut in half. Place chicken tips in a freezer bag and freeze to use for stock. Place wing pieces in a large rectangular baking dish that's been greased lightly or lined with parchment paper. You will have 24 wing pieces. Sprinkle lightly with additional sea salt and black pepper, place in the oven, and bake, turning over at 30-minute mark. Baste chicken wings with natural juices in pan. Brush mustard sauce all over wings, sprinkle with paprika and continue to cook for an additional 25–30 minutes until done. Wings should have an internal temperature of 165° F when done. ✑

MOLE CHILI

Serves 6–8

I love a good chili, especially when the weather is cold or rainy. This chili has a spicy, smoky flavor that comes from the combination of chipotle and Ancho chili powder. I call this chili a mole chili because it has the addition of cacao, cinnamon, and ground chili peppers which are key ingredients in mole sauce.

2-pounds organic grass-fed ground beef chuck or ground bison or 4 cups chopped Portobello mushrooms

½ cup diced peeled white onion

3 stalks organic celery—diced

½ organic green bell pepper— ribs and seeds removed and diced

4 teaspoons unrefined sea salt

2 teaspoons garlic powder

4 tablespoons Ancho chili powder

2 tablespoons raw cacao powder or unsweetened cocoa powder

¼ teaspoon pure vanilla extract

2 teaspoons ground cumin

¼ teaspoon cinnamon

¼ teaspoon fresh ground black pepper

½ teaspoon chipotle chili powder

1 (28-ounce) can organic ground peeled tomatoes

2 tablespoons organic tomato paste

3 cups Eden Foods canned organic black beans—rinsed and drained

4 cups filtered or spring water

¼ cup coconut sugar or Rapadura

In large stock pot with lid, add ground beef, ground bison, or mushrooms, onion, celery, bell pepper, sea salt, and garlic powder. Cook over medium heat until meat is brown and vegetables are soft, stirring to break up large chunks of ground meat. Remove from heat, place lid on pot, and drain off the fat if using meat. Place pot back on the stove and stir in remaining ingredients. Cook over medium-low heat for 45 minutes if vegan or 1 to 2 hours if using meat, stirring occasionally until chili is thick and full of flavor. Taste and adjust seasoning if needed. ᗡ

BEEF RAGU

Serves 4

This meat sauce is rich and deeply flavored from slowly simmering over low heat. Feel free to use bison in this recipe for a delicious alternative to beef.

1½-pounds organic grass-fed ground beef chuck

⅓ cup peeled white onion—finely chopped

⅓ cup organic celery ribs—finely chopped

¼ cup organic red or orange bell pepper— ribs and seeds removed and finely chopped

4 small cloves peeled garlic—minced

2 teaspoons unrefined sea salt

2 teaspoons dried oregano

⅛ teaspoon red chili flakes

2 tablespoons coconut sugar or Rapadura

¼ teaspoon fresh ground black pepper

4 cups puréed fresh roma tomatoes—seeds and skin removed or 1 large jar marinara or tomato basil sauce (Eden Foods or Cadia is a good choice)

2 tablespoons organic tomato paste

1 bay leaf

3 tablespoons fresh minced basil leaves

In 12-inch skillet, cook ground beef, onion, celery, and bell pepper on medium-high heat. Add minced garlic during last 2 minutes of cooking. Drain fat off meat and vegetables. Sprinkle meat mixture with sea salt, oregano, chili flakes, sweetener, and black pepper. Pour tomatoes or marinara sauce over meat mixture and stir in tomato paste. Add ¼ cup water if using fresh tomatoes, then add bay leaf and place on stovetop on medium-low heat. Simmer sauce covered for 40–60 minutes stirring occasionally. Add fresh basil during last 15 minutes of cooking. Taste and add more sea salt to taste if needed. Serve with quinoa or brown rice pasta or over roasted vegetables like spaghetti squash, fennel, or zucchini. ✑

VARIATION: VEGETABLE MARINARA

Substitute 1 cup zucchini chopped into 1-inch thick cubes and 2 cups chopped Portobello mushrooms for ground beef. Sauté in 2 tablespoons of olive oil with onion, celery, and bell pepper and proceed with recipe. ✑

LAMB CHOPS WITH SPICY MINT CHUTNEY

Serves 4

I love Indian food so I decided to create this lamb dish with all my favorite Indian flavors. Marinating the lamb in yogurt tenderizes it and adds great flavor.

MARINADE

½ teaspoon turmeric

⅔ cup organic plain yogurt

3 teaspoons curry powder

1 teaspoon fresh peeled ginger—grated

¼ teaspoon cinnamon

1 teaspoon peeled garlic cloves—grated

½ teaspoon smoked Spanish paprika

1 teaspoon unrefined sea salt

½ teaspoon cumin

1 teaspoon raw honey

8 pasture-raised loin lamb chops

Organic unsalted clarified butter—to cook lamb in

Place spices in a rectangular glass dish with remaining marinade ingredients except for lamb chops and clarified butter, and stir with spoon to blend well. Place lamb chops in marinade. Using your clean hands, coat lamb chops in yogurt marinade, making sure all lamb is totally coated. Cover dish and place lamb chops in refrigerator to marinate overnight or for at least 2 hours. Remove lamb chops from refrigerator and let lamb sit at room temperature for 15 minutes before cooking. Prepare spicy mint chutney on page 184 right before cooking lamb.

Place a grill pan or cast iron skillet on the stove and get hot on medium-high heat. Brush pan with butter and heat butter until it gets hot. Wipe excess marinade off lamb chops and place chops in hot pan. Cook lamb chops to 135° F for around 3–4 minutes per side for medium rare, depending on thickness. Serve with spicy mint chutney.

SPICY MINT CHUTNEY

Makes around ½ cup

1½ cups fresh mint leaves

½ cup fresh cilantro leaves

1 teaspoon raw honey

1 tablespoon fresh lime juice

½ serrano or jalapeño chili

¼ teaspoon unrefined sea salt

¼ cup green onions—rough chop

Prepare chutney right before cooking lamb. Place all ingredients for chutney in food processor and pulse until smooth. Taste and add more sea salt if needed. Set aside while you cook the lamb chops.

SLOW BRAISED BEEF ROAST

Serves 4

Slow cooking by braising is an excellent way to prepare tougher cuts of meat. Braising in a slow cooker is an easy method that is almost foolproof. Searing the meat before braising helps to caramelize the meat's outside and seal in the juices. Adding the plantain adds additional richness and body to the sauce.

3- to 4-pound organic grass-fed beef chuck roast

Unrefined sea salt and fresh ground black pepper

½ teaspoon paprika

2 tablespoons organic unsalted clarified butter

1 cup merlot or pinot noir

3 tablespoons organic tomato paste

1 ripe plantain—peeled and mashed

3 organic carrots—sliced in 2- to 3-inch pieces

2 organic celery ribs—sliced in 2- to 3-inch pieces

2 medium white onions—cut in half and sliced in ¼-inch pieces

5 cloves peeled garlic—cut into slices

2 teaspoons unrefined sea salt

3 cups beef stock (recipe on page 128)

1 large bay leaf

Sprinkle the roast to taste with sea salt, black pepper, and paprika. Heat clarified butter in skillet over medium high heat add roast and sear the meat on both sides until brown around 3 minutes per side. Remove the beef roast from the skillet drain off fat drippings and add wine, tomato paste, and plantains to the pan scraping up any brown bits with a spoon. Cook for 2 minutes before removing from heat. Place plantain and tomato paste mixture with beef drippings, and the remaining ingredients in the bottom of the slow cooker and stir to mix. Place beef on top of vegetables and baste with the sauce. Cover and cook on low for 7–8 hours until tender. Remove meat when done and cover with foil to keep warm. Puree cooked vegetables and braising liquid with immersion hand blender into a smooth sauce. Taste and adjust seasoning. Serve roast with sauce. ✍

CARROT WALNUT CREAM FETTUCCINE

Serves 4

CARROTS make wonderful raw noodles that are sweet and delicate. I have paired them with a carrot walnut cream sauce that adds enzyme-rich carrot juice and healthy fat from walnut butter. Enjoy this raw vegan entrée with a wonderful soup and salad for a filling, energy-filled vegan meal.

5–6 large organic carrots—washed and peeled

2 tablespoons fresh orange juice

2 tablespoons extra virgin olive oil

½ teaspoon unrefined sea salt

CARROT WALNUT CREAM SAUCE

½ cup fresh organic carrot juice

½ cup sprouted or raw walnut butter

1 medium orange—peeled and white pith removed

1 pinch fresh nutmeg

½ teaspoon unrefined sea salt

2 tablespoons flat-leaf parsley

Slice carrots into long ribbons with a vegetable peeler and stop before you reach the core. Save cores for stock or smoothies. Mix together orange juice, olive oil, and sea salt. Place carrot ribbons in a bowl and toss with this mixture. Cover and set aside to soften for at least 1 hour. Make the carrot walnut sauce after the carrot ribbons have had a chance to soften. Place all the sauce ingredients in a blender with the exception of the parsley leaves and puree until smooth and creamy. Taste and adjust seasoning. Drain liquid off the carrot noodles and toss with enough carrot walnut cream sauce to coast noodles. Sprinkle with fresh parsley and serve immediately.

*Raw Vegan

BASIL ALFREDO WITH ZUCCHINI NOODLES

Serves 2

This raw pasta is a play on traditional pasta for vegan eaters. The fresh basil and tomatoes add an authentic Italian flavor to the pasta. This entrée is great on hot summer nights when you want something quick, easy, and delicious without turning on the oven or stove. Nutritional yeast can be found in most health food stores and adds a cheese flavor to the Alfredo sauce.

¾ cup raw cashew nuts—soaked for 1 hour, rinsed, and drained well

1 small avocado—peeled and seed removed

½ cup plus 2 tablespoons purified water

2¼ teaspoons fresh lemon juice

¼ teaspoon lemon zest

1 clove peeled garlic—stem removed and grated

1 tablespoon nutritional yeast—optional but adds more cheese flavor

⅛ teaspoon cayenne pepper

2 teaspoons unrefined sea salt

Freshly ground black pepper—to taste

3 medium zucchini—peeled and sliced into long ribbons with a vegetable peeler

10 fresh basil leaves

1 cup chopped heirloom or roma tomatoes

Place all ingredients except zucchini, 4 basil leaves, and tomatoes in blender and blend until creamy and smooth. Taste and add more sea salt and black pepper to taste.

Toss sauce with raw zucchini pasta and top each plate with ½ cup chopped tomatoes and fresh torn basil leaves. ✑

HELFUL TIP TO MAKE GARLIC MILDER

Cut garlic bulb in half and remove thin stem in the center of each half to make the garlic milder.

---

*Raw Vegan

SUCCULENT SIDE DISHES

MY "SUCCULENT SIDE DISHES" INCLUDE VIBRANT VEGETABLES, WHOLE GRAINS, AND BEANS. I LIKE TO DO COMBINATIONS OF THESE SIDE DISHES SEVERAL TIMES PER WEEK.

FOR EXAMPLE, BROWN RICE PILAF, BLACK-EYED PEAS, AND MUSTARD AND TURNIP GREENS WITH ROASTED BABY TURNIPS MAKE A TOTALLY SATISFYING AND FILLING MEATLESS MEAL.

IF YOU SHOP AT THE LOCAL FARMERS' MARKET OR ARE A MEMBER OF A LOCAL COMMUNITY-SUPPORTED AGRICULTURE GROUP, FEEL FREE TO SUBSTITUTE THE PRODUCE YOU RECEIVE OR WHAT THE FARMERS RECOMMEND AT YOUR LOCAL MARKETS TO CREATE VARIATIONS OF THE SIDES THAT I HAVE CREATED.

WHEN MAKING THE GRAIN RECIPES, BE SURE TO SOAK THE GRAINS FIRST TO REMOVE THE PHYTIC ACID AND ENZYME INHIBITORS BEFORE COOKING. SOAK THE GRAINS IN WARM WATER WITH LEMON JUICE, RAW APPLE CIDER VINEGAR, OR WHEY ADDED. DOING THIS STEP ALSO MAKES THE GRAINS EASIER TO DIGEST AND RELEASES IMPORTANT NUTRIENTS.

BROWN RICE PILAF

Serves 6–8

Brown rice is a nutty, very nutritious, gluten-free grain that contains protein, iron, selenium, fiber, and B vitamins. Brown rice is low in phytic acid so if you don't have the time to soak it, just cook unsoaked rice in a mineral-rich stock. Cooking the rice with chicken stock adds delicious flavor and additional minerals and gelatin, all of which aid digestion, help boost the immune system, and help protect the body against disease. Feel free to use a rice cooker if you have one, because it is easy to use and makes great rice with little effort on your part.

2 cups long grain basmati brown rice—soaked for 2 hours in purified water with 4 tablespoons fresh lemon juice, raw apple cider vinegar, or whey added

2 tablespoons extra virgin olive oil or organic unsalted butter

1 small peeled yellow onion—diced

¼ cup organic celery ribs—diced

2 cloves peeled garlic—grated

1 bay leaf

4 cups homemade or low-sodium organic chicken stock

½ teaspoon unrefined sea salt

⅛ teaspoon fresh ground black pepper

2 tablespoons fresh minced basil or sorrel leaves

Drain and rinse rice well. In medium saucepan with lid, heat olive oil or butter on medium heat. Add drained rice, onion, celery ribs, and garlic. Cook over medium heat until rice begins to turn milky and vegetables turn soft. Add bay leaf, chicken stock, sea salt, and black pepper. Stir to combine and bring rice pilaf to a boil. Reduce heat, cover, and simmer on low heat until done, around 40–50 minutes. Stir minced basil or sorrel leaves into cooked rice and serve immediately. ᴗ

BLACK OR WILD RICE PILAF

Substitute black or wild rice for the brown rice and follow the rest of the recipe. Lotus Foods or Wilderness Family Farms is a good choice for the black rice.

POTATO PARSLEY MASH

Serves 4

ORGANIC POTATOES are an extremely satisfying and inexpensive vegetable that can be prepared in a variety of different ways. Organic potatoes are a good source of B vitamins, vitamin C, iron, and potassium. This rustic potato mash features Yukon Gold potatoes, which have an amazing, buttery taste and creamy texture which are great in this recipe. Other great potatoes to try are purple or red potatoes. Potatoes are a starchy vegetable, so eat with a healthy source of fat for slower absorption. Reserve potato skin peels to use in vegetable stock.

4 medium organic Yukon gold potatoes—washed, peeled, and cut into large cubes

3 tablespoons organic unsalted butter or roasted garlic olive oil

⅓ cup flat-leaf parsley—finely minced

2 teaspoons unrefined sea salt

½ teaspoon fresh ground black pepper

Place potatoes in a steamer basket pot with a steamer insert and sit inside of pot filled with 2–3 inches of water. Make sure water level does not come up to the steamer basket. Cover pot with top and steam potatoes over boiling water on medium-high heat until tender, around 35–45 minutes. Prick potatoes with fork to check for doneness. Potatoes should be soft when done cooking. Drain water out of pot and place hot potatoes in bottom of pot; mash potatoes with potato masher or large fork, and mix with butter or garlic olive oil, parsley, sea salt, and black pepper. Taste and adjust seasoning if needed. Serve immediately or cover with pot top and keep hot until ready to serve.

*Vegan if made with olive oil

SHITAKE MUSHROOM SAUTÉ

Serves 4

In Asia, shitake mushrooms are considered a healthy longevity food. One of the main reasons for this reputation is due to a compound called lentinan. Lentinan has been proven to strengthen the immune system, which protects the body against disease. This yummy shitake mushroom sauté is great served with brown rice pilaf and a green salad for a satisfying vegan meal.

2-pounds shitake mushrooms

2 tablespoons organic unsalted clarified butter or avocado oil

¼ cup chardonnay wine

Unrefined sea salt—to taste

Fresh ground black pepper—to taste

Remove mushroom stems and reserve to use in stock. Clean dirt from mushrooms caps. Cut in ½-inch slices and set aside. In large skillet, heat butter or avocado oil over medium-high heat until hot but not smoking. Add mushrooms slices in a single layer in pan and toss to coat with butter or avocado oil. Sauté mushrooms until they start to get soft for around 3–5 minutes. Remove pan from heat and add wine, continue to cook until mushrooms are tender and wine is reduced to a glaze which coats the mushrooms. Season mushrooms to taste with sea salt and fresh ground black pepper. Serve mushrooms hot.

*Vegan if made with avocado oil

BASIL GARLIC SPINACH

Serves 4

SPINACH is one of my top choices for vegetables. I eat it at least 2–3 times per week, either cooked or raw. Baby spinach is tender, delicate, and filled with iron, carotenoids, chlorophyll, folic acid, B vitamins, vitamin E, vitamin K, and vitamin C. These remarkable qualities are probably why Popeye was always eating his spinach!

2 tablespoons organic unsalted butter

6 cups organic baby spinach—rinsed and drained

¼ cup basil leaves—lightly chopped

1 teaspoon peeled garlic cloves—minced

1 teaspoon fresh lemon juice

Unrefined sea salt to taste

Fresh ground black pepper to taste

Heat butter in a 12-inch skillet or sauté pan over medium heat. Add spinach, basil, garlic, and lemon juice, and sprinkle with sea salt and black pepper to taste. Cook spinach, stirring frequently, until wilted and tender, around 4–5 minutes. Serve immediately.

VEGAN VERSION

Substitute avocado oil or olive oil for the butter and proceed with recipe.

GARLIC COLLARD GREENS

Makes around 4 servings

COLLARD GREENS are one of my favorite vegetables. I have loved them since I was a little girl. Most Southerners prepare their greens by slow cooking for hours with a smoked piece of meat until the greens are very soft. My new favorite way to enjoy greens is quickly cooked to lock in their fresh flavor and vibrant green color. When making this sauté, look for small, tender collard green leaves. If you use larger greens you will need to blanch the greens for around 10 minutes before sautéing. Collard greens are a cruciferous vegetable that is a potent cancer fighter and is high in phytochemicals, vitamins, minerals, and fiber. If you don't like garlic, feel free to leave it out.

Three bunches of collard greens (6 cups)

2 tablespoons organic unsalted clarified butter or avocado oil

¼ cup chardonnay wine

2 tablespoons spring or filtered water

Sea salt to taste

¼ teaspoon fresh ground black pepper

1 teaspoon coconut sugar or Rapadura

2 teaspoons peeled garlic cloves—minced

Remove ribs from collard greens, stack 4 or 5 leaves on top of each other, roll into a tight cylinder, and slice lengthwise into thin chiffonade or ribbons. Place cut greens in sterilized sink filled with water and clean dirt off thoroughly. This may take several changes of water. Transfer greens to a strainer or salad spinner and allow water to drain off. Heat butter or avocado oil in a large sauté pan on medium-high heat until hot but not smoking, and add greens, wine, water, sea salt, black pepper, and sweetener; stir together and cook for 15–20 minutes or until tender. Add garlic during the last 3 minutes of cooking time and stir well to incorporate garlic throughout the greens. Taste and adjust seasoning if needed and serve immediately. ✎

VEGAN VERSION

Substitute avocado oil or olive oil for the butter and proceed with recipe.

ZUCCHINI ONION SAUTÉ

Serves 4

I CREATED THIS SAUTÉ to highlight refreshing summer zucchini squash. I love the combination of zucchini paired with the onions and Tamari. Zucchini are packed with carotenes, hydrating water, vitamin C, and potassium. Zucchini is also very low in calories and is filling, which is good for anyone who is watching his or her caloric intake.

3 medium zucchini—washed and ends removed

2 tablespoons roasted garlic olive oil or extra virgin olive oil

1 small white onion—peeled and sliced in rings

1 tablespoon organic Nama® Shoyu soy sauce or wheat-free Tamari*

¼ teaspoon fresh ground black pepper

Thinly slice zucchini with a Mandoline or chef's knife. Heat skillet over medium heat until hot and add oil, zucchini, and onions to pan, sprinkle with Nama® Shoyu or Tamari and black pepper. Sauté the vegetables on medium heat for around 5–7 minutes until tender.

*You can substitute ½ teaspoon of unrefined sea salt for the Tamari or Nama® Shoyu soy sauce.

*Vegan

PURPLE CAULIFLOWER MASH

Serves 3–4

PURPLE CAULIFLOWER is a variety of cauliflower that has a vivid purple color and the same mild flavor as white cauliflower. The vivid purple color is from the antioxidant anthocyanin. I love to enjoy this purple variety raw and steamed. Seek out purple cauliflower at your local farmers market and you won't be disappointed. Cauliflower is a cruciferous vegetable that is a potent cancer fighter and contains antioxidants, vitamin K, potassium, B vitamins, and vitamin C. Drizzle with cultured cream for another tasty variation of this dish.

1 large head purple cauliflower—separated into florets, rinsed well

2 tablespoons organic cultured or regular unsalted butter

Unrefined sea salt to taste

Fresh ground black pepper to taste

Pour around 2 inches of water into bottom of saucepan with steamer insert or steamer basket. Place cauliflower in steamer and steam florets covered in pan on medium-high heat until tender, around 10–15 minutes. Drain water out of pan and place cauliflower into it. Place pan on stovetop and add butter. Mash cauliflower using a large fork or a potato masher. Season the cauliflower to taste with sea salt and black pepper. Remove from heat. Serve immediately.

VEGAN VERSION

Substitute avocado or extra virgin olive oil for the butter

SLOW-COOKED BLACK-EYED PEAS

Serves 6

BLACK-EYED PEAS and all beans were a staple food in our home. My mom would prepare them with smoked ham hocks or smoked turkey and cook them until tender and creamy. Our beans were always served with corn bread or corn pancakes, slices of tomatoes, and green onions. I have adapted my mom's recipe, using chicken stock, paprika, and chipotle for the smokiness instead of smoked meat. The chicken stock adds minerals and gelatin, which aids in the digestion of the bean's protein. Soaking the beans overnight in water neutralizes the enzyme inhibitors and phytic acid, which allows the beans nutrients to be more available to the body and aids in better digestion. Black-eyed peas are a great source of protein, vitamin A, calcium, and fiber, so eat up! If you experience gas when eating beans, cook them with a 3-inch piece of Kombu seaweed.

2 cups dried black-eyed peas

1 medium peeled white onion—cut into medium dice

4 peeled garlic cloves—grated

2 teaspoons coconut sugar or Rapadura

½ teaspoon fresh ground pepper

¾ teaspoon chipotle chili powder

1 teaspoon smoked sweet paprika

2 teaspoons raw apple cider vinegar

2 bay leaves

4–6 cups chicken stock (recipe on page 127)

Unrefined sea salt—add during last ½ hour

Place beans in a bowl, sort through them, and throw away any stones or shriveled beans. Rinse beans several times in cold water and drain. Add enough fresh cold water to cover the beans by 3 inches, cover bowl, and let sit at room temperature overnight. The next day drain and rinse the beans and place in the slow cooker or in a large pot. Add remaining ingredients except sea salt and add enough chicken stock to cover the beans by 2 inches and stir to combine. Cover with top and cook in slow cooker on high for 4 hours or bring to a boil on the stove top on high, skim off foam, and reduce to medium heat, cover and cook for 2 hours or until tender. Stir occasionally if cooking by stove top and add additional stock if needed. During the last half hour, season beans to taste with sea salt.

MUSTARD AND TURNIP GREENS WITH ROASTED BABY TURNIPS

Serves 6

GREENS were a favorite food in our home. My grandparents grew collards, mustards, and turnip greens, so we always had an abundance of tasty, healthy, leafy greens to enjoy. This recipe combines my favorite tender mustard and turnip greens and braises them quickly in stock.

10 baby turnips

3 tablespoons avocado oil or extra virgin olive oil

Unrefined sea salt and fresh ground black pepper to taste

2 large bunches turnip greens (4 cups)

2 large bunches mustard greens (4 cups)

4 peeled garlic cloves—minced

1 small dried chipotle chili pepper—seeds and stems removed and diced

1 medium peeled white onion—diced

1 tablespoon raw apple cider vinegar

2 teaspoons coconut sugar or Rapadura

2 tablespoons white wine

4 cups chicken or vegetable stock

Preheat oven to 400° F. Trim the roots from the top of the turnips, peel, and cut in half. Place turnips on baking sheet, toss with 2 tablespoons of oil, and sprinkle with sea salt and black pepper to taste. Spread turnips into a single layer and roast for 35–40 minutes until tender. Stir turnips about every 20 minutes to ensure even cooking. When done, remove from oven and cover with foil to keep warm. While turnips are cooking, prepare the greens. Remove ribs from greens, stack 4 or 5 leaves on top of each other, roll into a tight cylinder, and slice lengthwise into thin chiffonade or ribbons. Place cut greens in a clean sterilized sink filled with cold water and clean dirt off thoroughly. This may take several changes of water. Transfer greens to a strainer or salad spinner and allow water to drain off. Heat 1 tablespoon of oil on medium heat in a large pot and add minced garlic, chipotle pepper, and onions. Cook for 2 minutes, stirring frequently so vegetables don't burn. Add greens and sprinkle with apple cider vinegar, sweetener of choice, sea salt, and black pepper to taste. Add wine and stock of choice, cover and cook for 45–60 minutes or until tender. Taste and adjust seasoning if needed. Serve greens topped with roasted turnips.*Vegan if made with vegetable stock

POMEGRANATE MILLET PILAF

Serves 4

Many people recognize millet as a food for birds, but it is a extremely popular diet staple around the world. Millet is a good source of amino acids, B vitamins, magnesium, and fiber. It is an extremely versatile, gluten-free grain and has a mild, nutty flavor that tastes great in this pilaf. My favorite organic brand is by Eden Foods. The addition of tart and sweet ruby red pomegranate seeds adds great flavor, color, additional nutrients, and texture to this pilaf. You could also use chopped dried figs, golden raisins, dried cranberries, or dried cherries.

1 cup organic millet—soaked for 2 hours or overnight in purified water with 2 tablespoons fresh lemon juice, whey, or raw apple cider vinegar added

1 tablespoon organic unsalted clarified butter or extra virgin olive oil

⅓ cup peeled red onion—diced

½ cup organic celery—diced

3 cups chicken stock or vegetable stock

¼ teaspoon lemon juice

¼ teaspoon unrefined sea salt

⅛ teaspoon fresh ground black pepper

½ cup pomegranate seeds

Rinse and drain soaked millet thoroughly. Heat clarified butter or olive oil in a sauce pan over medium heat and add rinsed and drained millet, red onion, and celery. Cook millet and vegetables until millet is lightly toasted and vegetables are soft. Add remaining ingredients except pomegranate seeds, cover pan, and cook over medium heat for 30 minutes. Remove from heat, stir in pomegranate seeds, and serve immediately. ᴄ

HELPFUL TIP FOR REMOVING POMEGRANATE SEEDS

Cut pomegranate in half. Place a bowl in front of you and hold the cut side of the pomegranate half down. Hit the back of the pomegranate half with a large spoon until all the seeds fall out into the bowl. Discard the white pith and outer skin.

---

*Vegan if made with vegetable stock and olive oil

BARBECUE SWEET POTATO FRIES

Serves 4

SWEET POTATOES are high in carotenes, potassium, vitamin B6, vitamin C, biotin, and fiber. Baking the sweet potato fries with the barbecue spice blend creates a smoky, spicy, barbecue-flavored potato that is healthier and better tasting than any store-bought barbecue potato chip.

BARBECUE SPICE BLEND

1 teaspoon chipotle powder

2 teaspoons smoked sweet paprika

¼ teaspoon cumin

½ teaspoon garlic powder

¼ teaspoon onion powder

1 tablespoon coconut sugar or Rapadura

½ teaspoon unrefined sea salt

⅛ teaspoon cinnamon

¼ teaspoon fresh ground black pepper

SWEET POTATOES

2 large sweet potatoes or red garnet yams—washed and peeled

3 tablespoons melted virgin coconut oil or olive oil

Preheat oven to 400° F. Line a large baking sheet with parchment paper or lightly grease pan. In small bowl mix together spice blend ingredients. Set aside to use later. Cut washed sweet potatoes or yams into 1-inch french fries and coat with oil. Place potatoes in a single layer on baking sheet and bake them for 40–45 minutes until golden, tender, and slightly crispy. Turn halfway through the cooking time to ensure even browning. Sprinkle barbecue spice blend over fries during last 20 minutes of cooking and toss to coat well. Remove from oven when done and serve immediately. Sweet potatoes and yams have higher water content than yellow potatoes, so they won't be as crispy.

*Vegan

ROASTED LEMON FENNEL AND ONIONS

Serves 4

I love roasting fennel and onions. Once you roast fennel and onions, they become sweeter, milder, and caramelized with a lush, melting texture. The roasted lemon adds an additional citrus flavor note that really enhances the fennel. Enjoy this vegetable dish with fish or topped with meat ragu.

3 Fennel bulbs—reserve 1 teaspoon fennel fronds*

1 large white onion—peeled and cut into ½-inch slices

⅓ cup extra virgin olive oil

¾ teaspoon unrefined sea salt

⅛ teaspoon fresh ground black pepper

1 medium lemon—sliced in half

Preheat oven to 400° F. Remove stalks from the top of the fennel bulb, remove tough outer layer, and reserve 1 teaspoon of the fennel fronds. Slice dark bottom off of the fennel, slice bulb in half, and remove core. Thinly slice the fennel halves vertically with a knife or on the Mandoline into ½-inch slices. Place fennel slices, onion slices, and lemon halves in large baking pan. Toss vegetables with olive oil, sea salt, and black pepper until well coated. Roast vegetables and lemon in the oven until tender and caramelized, around 35–40 minutes. Turn vegetables over after 20 minutes. Remove from oven and squeeze roasted lemon halves over vegetables, sprinkled with reserved fennel fronds and serve immediately.

*Fennel fronds are the leafy green tops of the fennel. They have a wonderful light anise flavor. Taste and see if you like this flavor before sprinkling on top of the roasted vegetables. ✎

*Vegan

SUPER SNACKS

SUPER SNACKS ARE WONDERFUL TO EAT WHEN YOU ARE HUNGRY AND NOT READY TO EAT A FULL MEAL. SUPER SNACKS ARE ALSO FANTASTIC TO SERVE AT PARTIES AND WILL GIVE YOUR GUESTS HEALTHY AND DELICIOUS OPTIONS TO ENJOY. WHEN I AM TOO BUSY TO MAKE MY SUPER SNACKS, I ENJOY SNACKS THAT TAKE 5 MINUTES TO MAKE. THESE 5-MINUTE QUICK SNACKS ARE GREAT AND INCLUDE:

1. AVOCADO HALF SPRINKLED WITH SEA SALT AND CRACKED BLACK PEPPER OR MASHED AVOCADO WRAPPED IN NORI.

2. TOMATO SLICES DRIZZLED WITH OLIVE OIL AND SPRINKLED WITH TORN BASIL LEAVES AND SEA SALT.

3. OLIVES AND RAW ORGANIC CHEESE CUBES.

4. SPROUTED FLAX CRACKERS OR APPLE SLICES SERVED WITH SPROUTED OR RAW NUT OR SEED BUTTER.

5. CUCUMBER SLICES TOPPED WITH ORGANIC YOGURT AND FRESH DILL.

6. RADISHES SPREAD WITH CULTURED BUTTER AND SPRINKLED WITH SEA SALT.

7. ORGANIC GREEK YOGURT WITH FRESH FIGS AND RAW HONEY.

8. SPROUTED NUTS, SEEDS, AND DRIED FRUIT TOSSED TOGETHER.

SWEET POTATOES WITH COCONUT CINNAMON SPRINKLE

Serves 4

Whenever my mom made sweet potato pies, she would always bake a few extra potatoes so that we could have twice-cooked sweet potatoes for breakfast or a snack the next day. I love the contrast of the crispy, nutritionally dense sweet potato with the coconut flakes, coconut sugar, and cinnamon. Coconut sugar has a low glycemic index of 35 and an excellent nutritional profile that includes potassium, magnesium, iron, zinc, and B vitamins. These potatoes are great by themselves and make a great snack food. It's easier if you bake the potatoes the day before you want to make this recipe.

2 medium-sized sweet potatoes or red garnet yams—washed and patted dry

½ cup unsweetened dried coconut flakes

¼ cup coconut sugar

2 teaspoons cinnamon

Virgin coconut oil or organic unsalted clarified butter for pan

Preheat oven to 375° F. Place washed sweet potatoes in lightly greased baking pan. Pierce sweet potatoes all over with a fork. Bake in the oven for 45 minutes to 1 hour until potatoes are tender when touched. Remove potatoes from the oven and cool until room temperature. Place in refrigerator and chill until firm. Remove potatoes from refrigerator, peel, and slice into ¼-inch slices. In small bowl mix together coconut flakes, coconut sugar, and cinnamon and set aside. Heat a skillet on medium heat until hot. Add enough coconut oil or butter to coat bottom of skillet. Place sweet potato slices into skillet and cook until golden brown and crispy on the bottom, around 3–4 minutes. Flip potatoes over and continue cooking until golden brown and crispy on the other side. Drain on plate lined with a paper towel and sprinkle with the coconut cinnamon sprinkle. Serve warm.

VEGAN VERSION

Make with coconut oil.

SPICY GUACAMOLE

Makes around 3 cups

Avocados are an amazing fruit that is rich in potassium, heart-healthy monounsaturated fat, vitamin E, and B vitamins. This creamy, fresh guacamole makes a great snack that is nutritious and satisfying. Remove the seeds from the jalapeño if you want a milder guacamole. Experiment with substituting different herbs, such as basil and parsley, for the cilantro.

2 large avocados (2 cups)

2 small roma or heirloom tomatoes—finely chopped

3 tablespoons peeled diced red onion

Juice from 1 small lime

2 tablespoons fresh cilantro leaves—minced

1 minced jalapeño

⅛ teaspoon organic cayenne pepper

1 teaspoon organic cumin powder

2 cloves peeled garlic—minced

Unrefined sea salt to taste

Fresh ground black pepper to taste

⅓ cup Hemp seeds—optional

Halve and seed the avocados. Scoop out the flesh into a medium mixing bowl and, using a fork, mash well, leaving some avocados in chunks. Mix in remaining ingredients and stir well with a spoon. Taste and add more sea salt or black pepper if needed. Serve with cultured tomato pineapple salsa and baked organic tortilla chips, sliced vegetables, or lettuce leaves.

*Raw Vegan

SMOKY ORANGE HUMMUS

Makes around 2 cups

Hummus is one of my favorite ways to enjoy chickpeas. This easy and quick recipe uses fresh orange juice and orange zest along with canned garbanzo beans and smoked paprika for a new twist on the traditional recipe. Eden Organic canned beans are packed in BPA-free cans. Chickpeas are high in potassium, vitamin B9, and iron. The hummus has a beautiful light orange color and smoky flavor from the smoked paprika. Enjoy this fiber- and protein-rich hummus with sprouted flax crackers, olives, and raw vegetables.

1 (15-ounce) can Eden Organic garbanzo beans

3 tablespoons raw tahini

¼ cup fresh orange juice

1 tablespoon filtered water

½ teaspoon orange zest

⅓ cup O Blood orange olive oil or your favorite extra virgin olive oil

2 peeled minced garlic cloves

½ teaspoon cumin powder

¾ teaspoon unrefined sea salt

½ teaspoon smoked sweet paprika

Fresh ground black pepper to taste

Pour beans into a strainer and rinse thoroughly with water. Drain beans well and place in a food processor with S blade attachment. Add remaining ingredients, place lid on food processor, and blend until hummus is smooth and creamy. Stop processor to scrape down sides if needed. Taste hummus and add more seasoning if needed to taste. If hummus is too thick, add small amount of purified water 1 tablespoon at a time to get the right consistency. Enjoy immediately, drizzled with olive oil, or place in covered container in the refrigerator for up to 1 week. ᴄ

*Vegan

ENCRUSTED GOAT CHEESE

Makes around 1½ cups

THIS GOAT CHEESE is creamy, tangy, savory, and chewy. This vividly colored snack is wonderful to serve with brown rice crackers, flax crackers, nut crackers, sprouted bread, or raw vegetables. It is great as a starter for dinner parties and is always a big hit.

¾ cup finely chopped oven-dried tomatoes (recipe on page 60)

2 teaspoons cracked black or pink peppercorns

¼ cup extra virgin olive oil

1 (8-ounce) soft goat cheese log

Place tomatoes and cracked peppercorns in bowl and mix well to combine. Pour olive oil into a bowl big enough to hold the goat cheese log and roll goat cheese log in the olive oil until it is completely coated on all sides. Dip the goat cheese in the tomato peppercorn mixture until it is completely coated on all sides. Slice into ¼-inch slices or place in airtight covered container and refrigerate for up to 3 weeks. ☟

HELPFUL TIP FOR CRACKING PEPPERCORNS AND SLICING GOAT CHEESE

PLACE PEPPERCORNS in a small plastic bag and close. Use a mallet, rolling pin, or hammer to lightly crack peppercorns into smaller pieces. To easily slice goat cheese, use a long piece of clean dental floss and, holding both ends of floss, use it to cut goat cheese log into slices.

GOAT CHEESE TOPPING VARIATION

Substitute ¾ cup of sprouted or raw nuts or seeds for the oven-dried tomatoes and cracked peppercorns and proceed with recipe.

VEGAN VERSION

Substitute nut or seed cheese and follow recipe.

CULTURED VEGETABLE DIP

Makes around 1 cup

I MADE THIS CULTURED DIP for an anti-aging workshop and at a store demo for Rejuvenative Foods at Erewhon Natural Market. It was a big hit and everyone wanted the recipe. This yummy dip combines Rejuvenative Foods Vegi-Delite Zing raw cultured vegetables with almond butter for a smooth, creamy dip filled with probiotics, protein, healthy fats, enzymes, and fiber, which will aid digestion and help heal your digestive tract.

3 tablespoons Rejuvenative Foods Vegi-Delite Zing raw cultured vegetables
¼ cup O Blood orange extra virgin olive oil
2 tablespoons O Pomegranate vinegar
1 tablespoon raw or sprouted almond butter
1 tablespoon organic maple syrup—grade B

Blend all ingredients in a blender until smooth and creamy. Pour into small bowl and enjoy with fresh vegetables. ✎

*Raw Vegan

CAROB PECAN SPREAD

Makes around ½ cup

I ENJOY EATING different varieties of nut and seed butters for a healthy snack that keeps me satisfied for hours. I created this snack with creamy pecan butter and carob for an unforgettable taste sensation. Enjoy this spread with apple slices, pear slices, or on top of sprouted grain bread. If you don't have pecan butter, substitute whatever raw or sprouted nut or seed butter you have on hand. I like to use almond and cashew butter in this recipe also.

½ cup raw or sprouted pecan butter
2 tablespoons carob powder
2 teaspoons organic maple syrup—grade B
½ teaspoon cinnamon
1 teaspoon pure vanilla extract

In small bowl blend together all ingredients until thoroughly combined. Taste and add more carob or maple syrup to taste. Enjoy immediately or keep in covered container in the refrigerator for up to 2 weeks. ✎

*Raw Vegan

PUMPKIN SEED SPREAD

Makes around 2 cups

SEED OR NUT SPREADS are a great dairy-free alternative to soft cheese spreads. Starting with sprouted or raw nuts and seeds will give you the key nutrients and healthy fats your body requires on a daily basis. Enjoy this soft, creamy, vibrant green spread in lettuce leaves, with raw vegetables, or on sprouted grain bread or crackers.

1 cup sprouted or raw pumpkin seeds

¼ cup fresh lemon juice

2 cloves peeled garlic—grated

Unrefined sea salt to taste

1 small avocado—peeled and seed removed

¼ teaspoon cayenne pepper

Purified water if needed

Place pumpkin seeds in a food processor fitted with the S blade attachment. Place lid on and grind pumpkin seeds until seeds turn into a pumpkin seed butter. Add remaining ingredients except water and pulse until well combined and creamy. Add small amount of water if spread is too thick and continue to blend spread until smooth. Place spread in a covered container in the refrigerator for up to 3 days if not eating right away. ⌒

*Raw Vegan

CHIVE DEVILED EGGS

Serves 4

DEVILED EGGS are a family favorite. We enjoy them for breakfast, lunch, and snacks. I changed the family recipe by substituting plain Greek yogurt in place of mayonnaise, which creates a creamy egg full of healthy probiotics. Pastured eggs are a perfect source of budget-friendly protein. Pastured eggs contain a large amount of choline, which helps maintain integrity and flexibility in our cells and keeps our brain healthy and functioning properly.

6 large eggs

1 teaspoon unrefined sea salt

¼ teaspoon garlic powder

¼ teaspoon onion powder

⅛ teaspoon smoked sweet paprika

⅛ teaspoon cayenne pepper

⅛ teaspoon fresh ground black pepper

1 teaspoon Rapadura or pinch stevia

1½ teaspoons Dijon mustard

¼–⅓ cup organic plain Greek yogurt

2 tablespoons minced chives

Place eggs in a pan and cover with cold water. Bring the eggs to a boil over medium-high heat for 5 minutes. Turn off the heat and let eggs sit covered for 5 minutes in hot water. Remove the hot water, fill the pan with cold water, and cool for around 2 to 3 minutes. Remove eggs from shells and chop in half. Place egg yolks in a bowl, mash until smooth, and sprinkle with sea salt, garlic powder, onion powder, smoked paprika, cayenne pepper, and black pepper. Add sweetener of choice along with Dijon mustard and blend well. Add yogurt and mix together until creamy. Taste and adjust seasoning if needed. Stuff egg white halves with egg yolk filling. Sprinkle with chives and serve immediately or chill in the refrigerator until cold. ⌒

DELICIOUS DESSERTS

DELICIOUS DESSERTS CAN BE THE PERFECT ENDING TO A GREAT MEAL. IF SOMEONE IS NEW TO EATING VEGAN FOODS, THEN LET THEM TRY SOME OF THE DECADENT AND HEALTHY DESSERTS IN THIS SECTION AND THEY WILL BE SURPRISED AT HOW GREAT THEY ARE.

HEALTHY DESSERTS ARE NUTRIENT-RICH, AND YOU CAN FEEL SATISFIED WITH A SMALLER AMOUNT. I PERSONALLY LIKE TO ENJOY DESSERTS THAT SATISFY MY SWEET TOOTH WITHOUT MAKING ME FEEL TIRED AND TOO FULL.

ALL OF THESE DESSERTS WILL MAKE YOU FEEL HAPPY BECAUSE THEY ARE MADE WITHOUT THE USE OF REFINED WHITE FLOUR, REFINED WHITE SUGAR, HIGH FRUCTOSE CORN SYRUP, PRESERVATIVES, OR UNHEALTHY FATS. FEEL FREE TO INDULGE WITHOUT GUILT!

RAW CHOCOLATE MOUSSE

Makes around 2 cups

THIS RAW CHOCOLATE MOUSSE is rich and creamy without the addition of dairy or eggs. It is a great source of lauric acid, vitamins, and minerals from the coconut and protein, flavonoids, and fiber from the cacao and carob powder. The carob powder intensifies the flavor of the cacao and adds a nice touch of sweetness and caramel flavor that really elevates the mousse. If you can't find young coconut meat in your area, use 2 avocados in the recipe. I prefer Hass avocados in this recipe.

1 small avocado—peeled and seed removed

Coconut meat from 1 young coconut

3 tablespoons raw cacao powder

2 tablespoons carob powder

3 tablespoons organic maple syrup—grade B

¼ teaspoon cinnamon

1 teaspoon pure vanilla extract

Tiny pinch unrefined sea salt

Blend all ingredients in a food processor and pulse until smooth and creamy. Taste and add more cacao or maple syrup if you like a sweeter more chocolate mousse. Place in airtight container and chill for at least ½ hour before eating. ∽

*Raw Vegan

RASPBERRY CHOCOLATE MOUSSE PIE

Makes (1) 9-inch pie

THIS RASPBERRY CHOCOLATE MOUSSE PIE is delicious and perfect for entertaining. Your family and friends will be surprised to discover that this dessert is healthy when they try it.

1 cup unsweetened dried coconut flakes

2 packages Go Raw chocolate super cookies

¼ cup carob powder

1 teaspoon cinnamon

⅛ teaspoon unrefined sea salt

⅓ cup Medjool dates—pit and chop

½ teaspoon orange zest

2 tablespoons virgin coconut butter

1 double recipe raw chocolate mousse (recipe on page 214)

2 cups fresh Raspberries

In food processor pulse coconut flakes, cookies, carob, cinnamon, and sea salt until mixture looks like fine crumbs. Add dates, orange zest, and coconut butter and pulse until mixture starts to hold together. Add tiny amount of water if crust is not sticking together. Spoon the crust into a greased 9-inch pie pan or springform pan, grease your hands with coconut butter, and press crust on bottom and sides of pan evenly. Freeze crust until firm. Spoon chocolate mousse on top of pie crust, spread evenly, and refrigerate for at least an hour. Garnish with fresh raspberries before serving.

*Raw Vegan

HOT FUDGE SAUCE

Makes around 2 cups

THIS HOT FUDGE SAUCE gets it heat from the cayenne pepper. This heat combined with the sweetness of the chocolate sauce makes a great flavor combination that is good with my strawberry frozen yogurt or with fresh fruit like bananas or strawberries. Cacao butter is the pure butter that is pressed from the cacao bean. It has a wonderful chocolate flavor and makes the chocolate sauce shiny and creamy.

¾ cup raw cacao powder

¼ cup carob powder

1 cup coconut nectar

¼ cup melted raw cacao butter or virgin coconut oil

½ teaspoon cinnamon

⅛ teaspoon unrefined sea salt

1 tablespoon pure vanilla extract or seeds from 1 vanilla bean

⅛ teaspoon organic cayenne pepper

Blend all ingredients in a blender until smooth. Enjoy immediately or place in glass jar with lid and store in refrigerator for 2 weeks. If refrigerated, warm sauce until it gets soft and pourable.

*Raw Vegan

FUDGE GOJI BERRY TRUFFLES

Makes around 10 truffles

1½ cups hot fudge sauce

½ cup finely chopped raw macadamia nuts (unsoaked)

¼ cup goji berries

½ cup sweetened cacao nibs—optional

Mix together fudge sauce, nuts, and goji berries in a small bowl until well combined. Cover and freeze for 2 hours. With a tablespoon or small ice cream scoop, scoop out chocolate, form into 2-inch balls with your hand, and roll balls in cacao nibs if using. Enjoy immediately or cover and freeze until ready to eat. Truffles will last for 2 weeks covered in the refrigerator. ⌒

*Raw Vegan

STRAWBERRY FROZEN YOGURT WITH BALSAMIC SYRUP

Makes around 2½ pints

I LOVE FROZEN YOGURT, so I created my own version using goat's milk yogurt. This frozen strawberry yogurt is sweet, creamy, tangy, and luscious. The balsamic syrup adds a unique twist that elevates the flavor of the strawberries and yogurt. If you can't find goat yogurt, feel free to substitute organic whole cow's milk plain yogurt.

1 (32-ounce) container Redwood Hill Farm plain goat's yogurt or organic whole cow's milk yogurt

16 ounces fresh strawberries—green stems removed and cut in half

½–¾ cup coconut sugar or ⅛ teaspoon or 1 packet stevia

Seeds from 1 vanilla bean or 1 tablespoon pure vanilla extract

Tiny pinch unrefined sea salt

Balsamic syrup—reserve to use later

Place a mesh strainer inside a larger bowl. Line the strainer with a thin, clean dish towel or tripled pieces of cheesecloth, and place the strainer over a bowl. Spoon the yogurt in towel or cheesecloth, cover, and let the yogurt sit in the refrigerator overnight until the whey drips into the bowl. Pour whey into glass jar with lid and place in refrigerator to use for making cultured vegetables or fruits. Place strawberries in the blender and add strained yogurt, ½ cup of coconut sugar or the stevia, vanilla, and pinch of sea salt, blending until smooth. Add more sweetener if needed to taste. Chill yogurt for at least ½ hour. Pour chilled yogurt into a chilled ice cream maker and freeze according to manufacturer's directions. Enjoy immediately drizzled with balsamic syrup, or store in an airtight container in the freezer. If you store the frozen yogurt in the freezer, make sure you place in refrigerator for 15 minutes to soften before eating because frozen yogurt will become very hard in the freezer. Frozen yogurt lasts for 4 weeks covered in the freezer. ✎

BALSAMIC SYRUP

You can create balsamic syrup with balsamic vinegar by placing ½ cup of balsamic vinegar in a small saucepan and cooking on medium-low heat until reduced to a syrup consistency that coats the back of a spoon. Make sure to stir occasionally while reducing into the syrup. My favorite balsamic to use with this ice cream is O Port Balsamic vinegar. All of O's Balsamic vinegars are slowly aged in oak barrels. This balsamic syrup is great to drizzle on this frozen yogurt and on salads, fresh tomatoes, cooked mushrooms, and fresh strawberries. ✎

PIÑA COLADA ICE CREAM

Makes around 3 pints

Piña coladas are a very popular tropical drink made with coconut, pineapple, and rum. I decided to create a decadent ice cream with these flavors without the use of alcohol. Enjoy this ice cream on a warm summer day and imagine yourself relaxing on the beach with a tropical breeze gently fanning you.

3 cups fresh pineapple cubes

2¾ cups full-fat unsweetened coconut milk—preservative free

½ cup raw coconut nectar or coconut sugar

1½ teaspoons pure vanilla extract

Tiny pinch unrefined sea salt

1 cup dried unsweetened coconut flakes—optional

Place pineapple in a high-speed blender and blend until smooth. Strain pineapple puree through a fine mesh strainer into a bowl using the back of a large spoon to push puree through strainer. Place strained puree back in blender and add remaining ingredients except coconut and blend until smooth and creamy. Taste and add more sweetener if needed. Mix in coconut if using and chill ice cream for at least ½ hour. Pour chilled ice cream into a chilled ice cream maker and freeze according to manufacturer's directions. If you don't own an ice cream maker, use frozen pineapple and chilled coconut milk and blend all ingredients in blender until creamy. Ice cream can be consumed immediately after blending. It will have the consistency of soft-serve ice cream. If you like it firmer, place in airtight containers and freeze until firm. If you store the ice cream in the freezer, make sure you place in refrigerator for 15 minutes to soften before eating because ice cream will become very hard in the freezer. Ice cream lasts for 3 weeks covered in the freezer. ᕦ

*Raw Vegan

PIÑA COLADA ICE CREAM FLOAT

Makes 2 servings

4 scoops of piña colada ice cream
2 cups coconut kefir

Place 2 scoops of ice cream into two tall glasses. Top each glass with coconut kefir, stir, and enjoy immediately. ᕦ

MANGO ICE CREAM

Makes around 3 pints

MANGOS are a very popular tropical fruit that makes a luscious, dairy-free ice cream when combined with creamy mango cashew milk. I decided to create a decadent ice cream with these flavors when I had an abundant of fresh mangos. Enjoy this ice cream whenever you want something sweet, cold, and creamy. You can also make a mango ice cream float by placing a scoop of ice cream in a glass and topping it off with my recipe for coconut kefir or mango kefir by Kevita.

3 cups fresh or frozen mango cubes

2¾ cups mango cashew milk (recipe on page 75)

2 drops essential orange oil or 2 tablespoons fresh orange juice

Tiny pinch unrefined sea salt

¼ cup raw coconut nectar or coconut sugar—optional

Place all ingredients except sweetener in a high-speed blender and blend until smooth and creamy. Taste and add sweetener if needed. Chill ice cream for at least ½ hour. Pour chilled ice cream into a chilled ice cream maker and freeze according to manufacturer's directions. Enjoy immediately. If you don't own an ice cream maker, use frozen mango and chilled mango cashew milk, and ice cream can be consumed immediately after blending. It will have the consistency of soft-serve ice cream. If you like it firmer, place in airtight containers and freeze until firm. If you store the ice cream in the freezer, make sure you place in refrigerator for 15 minutes to soften before eating because ice cream will become very hard in the freezer. Ice cream lasts for 3 weeks covered in the freezer. ✑

PAPAYA ICE CREAM

Substitute 3 cups fresh or frozen papaya for the mango. Remove the orange oil and add 1 teaspoon fresh lemon juice and 1 teaspoon of pure vanilla extract. Follow instructions for blending and freezing from the mango ice cream recipe. ✑

*Raw Vegan

BANANA COCONUT CHIA PUDDING

Makes around 2½ cups

Here is a yummy recipe for pudding featuring chia seeds one of my favorite superfoods. Make this dairy-free pudding whenever you want a quick and healthy dessert and your body will thank you for it!

1¼ cups full-fat unsweetened coconut milk —preservative free

2 large peeled bananas—organic or fair trade

1½ teaspoons pure vanilla extract

¼ cup organic maple syrup—grade B

¼ teaspoon nutmeg

½ teaspoon cinnamon

⅓ cup chia seeds

⅓ cup dried unsulfured banana chips

⅓ cup dried unsweetened large coconut flakes

Place coconut milk, peeled bananas, vanilla, maple syrup, nutmeg, and cinnamon in a blender and blend until smooth. Taste and add more maple syrup if you like it sweeter. Pour into a container with a lid and slowly stir in the chia seeds until well mixed. Let pudding sit at room temperature for 10 minutes. Stir pudding again, cover, and place in the refrigerator overnight. Top the pudding with dried banana chips and coconut flakes before serving. Pudding will last covered in the refrigerator for up to 10 days. ⌐

*Raw Vegan

DELICIOUSLY HOLISTIC

ACAI BERRY CRANBERRY TEA SHERBET

Makes around 2 pints

I love to use tea in a variety of different recipes to add wonderful flavor and fantastic health benefits. The tea I used for this dairy-free sherbet is Zhena's Gypsy Tea Acai Berry tea. This caffeine-free red tea is a delectable organic blend of Rooibos, rosehip, hibiscus, orange peel, lemongrass, Sambazon acai berry, essential oil of mandarin, and peach. This tea is an excellent source of antioxidants, vitamins, and minerals. I use the tea to infuse the creamy coconut milk and blend it with fresh tart red cranberries, banana, vanilla bean, and essential orange oil for an unforgettable taste sensation.

2½ cups full-fat unsweetened coconut milk—preservative free

Seeds and pod from 1 vanilla bean

¼ teaspoon cinnamon

Zhena's Gypsy Tea Acai Berry—use 2 tea sachets

1¼ cups coconut nectar or coconut sugar

4 drops essential orange oil

3 cups cranberries

1 small banana—organic or fair-trade

In medium saucepan add coconut milk, pod and seeds from 1 vanilla bean, and cinnamon and stir to combine. Bring mixture to a low simmer on medium heat. Once the milk is hot add tea sachets and stir. Turn heat to low and let tea steep for 3–5 minutes. Remove vanilla pod and tea sachets from coconut milk and stir in coconut nectar or coconut sugar and orange oil. Cool tea infused milk for around 10 minutes. Add cooled milk into blender container with cranberries and banana. Blend sherbet until smooth. Taste and add more sweetener if you like the sherbet sweeter. Strain sherbet thru fine-mesh strainer to remove any cranberry skin. Chill sherbet for at least 4 hours or overnight. Pour chilled sherbet into a chilled ice cream maker and freeze according to manufacturer's directions. Enjoy immediately. If you don't own an ice cream maker, chill the tea infused coconut milk and use frozen cranberries and banana. Blend ingredients in blender until smooth and sherbet can be consumed immediately after blending. It will have the consistency of soft-serve ice cream. If you like it firmer, place in airtight containers and freeze until firm. If you store the sherbet in the freezer, make sure you place in refrigerator for 15 minutes to soften before eating because sherbet will become very hard in the freezer. Sherbet lasts for 3 weeks covered in the freezer. ✎

*Vegan

DELICIOUSLY HOLISTIC

CAROB ALMOND CHIA PUDDING

Makes around 2 cups

CAROB ALMOND CHIA PUDDING is a delicious, nutrient-rich pudding that is healing to the digestive system and hydrating for your body. Chia seeds are an excellent source of omega-3 and 6 fatty acids, protein, antioxidants, calcium, and fiber. Chia is also a hydrophilic, or "water-loving," seed which holds up to many times its weight in water, which is great for preventing dehydration. When the chia seeds are soaked in the almond milk, they soften and swell which makes the pudding similar in texture to tapioca. Enjoy this easy to make pudding whenever you are craving tapioca. I like this pudding topped with fresh blueberries or dried cranberries.

1½ cups unsweetened almond milk

2 tablespoons sprouted or raw almond butter

¼ cup carob powder

1 teaspoon pure vanilla extract

⅓ cup organic maple syrup—grade B or 2 packets stevia

½ cup chia seeds

Fresh or dried fruit

Place almond milk, almond butter, carob, vanilla, and sweetener of choice in a blender and blend until smooth. Taste and add more sweetener if needed. Pour into a bowl, add chia seeds and stir until well mixed. Let pudding sit for 10 minutes at room temperature. Stir pudding again, cover, and place in the refrigerator overnight. Top the chia pudding with fresh or dried fruit before serving. Carob almond chia pudding will last for up to 14 days in the refrigerator.

*Raw Vegan

PLUM CRUMBLE

Serves 2

I LOVE FRUIT DESSERTS because they taste delicious and are filled with healthy ingredients that taste amazing when paired together. I created this plum crumble to showcase plums, which are one of my favorite stone fruits. Plums are sweet, juicy, and delicious, with a high amount of vitamin A. I have used walnuts for the topping, but feel free to substitute whatever nuts or seeds you have on hand.

PLUM FILLING

4 large plums—cut in half and pits removed

1 teaspoon fresh orange juice

2 teaspoons coconut sugar or 1 teaspoon raw honey

CRUMBLE TOPPING

1 cup raw or sprouted walnuts

8 chopped dried pitted plums (½ cup)

½ teaspoon cinnamon

⅛ teaspoon fresh ground nutmeg

Seeds from ½ vanilla bean

⅛ teaspoon unrefined sea salt

Thinly slice plums on a Mandoline or with a chef's knife and toss with orange juice and coconut sugar or honey. Set aside while you make the crumble topping. Place walnuts in food processor fitted with an S blade and pulse until walnuts are rough chopped. Don't over process or walnuts will turn into nut butter. Add remaining ingredients for the crumble topping and process until mixture starts to stick together and resemble coarse crumbs. Place plum slices in bottom of 2 bowls and top with crumble topping. Serve immediately.

*Raw Vegan

HELPFUL TIP FOR CUTTING DRIED PLUMS

RUB YOUR CHEF'S KNIFE with a small amount of oil before cutting dried plums or any dried fruit and the fruit will not stick to your knife.

PUMPKIN RAISIN HEMP BREAD PUDDING

Serves 10

RAISIN HEMP MILK

2 cups unsweetened hemp milk

¼ teaspoon unrefined sea salt

1 tablespoon pure vanilla extract or seeds from 1 vanilla bean

¼ cup dark raisins

Place all ingredients for raisin hemp milk in a high-speed blender and blend until smooth and creamy. Reserve the raisin hemp milk to use in pumpkin hemp custard. ⤸

*Raw Vegan

PUMPKIN HEMP CUSTARD

2 cups raisin hemp milk

1¾ cups cooked pumpkin purée

¾ cup organic maple syrup—grade B

1½ teaspoons cinnamon

¼ teaspoon nutmeg

⅛ teaspoon ginger

1 large egg

2 teaspoons virgin coconut oil

2 loaves Manna Organics Banana Walnut Hemp Bread—defrosted and cut into 1-inch cubes

½ cup dark raisins

Place all custard ingredients except egg, coconut oil, bread cubes, and raisins in blender and blend until smooth. Taste and add more maple syrup if you like it sweeter. Add egg and blend for another 30 seconds to incorporate in custard. Grease a 9x13-inch baking pan with 2 teaspoons of coconut oil. Place bread cubes and raisins in pan and toss to mix together. Pour the hemp pumpkin custard over the bread and raisins and stir together. Cover bread pudding and let sit for 40 minutes to allow custard to soften bread cubes. Preheat oven to 325° F. Place bread pudding in the oven and bake for 50 to 60 minutes or until the custard has set and pudding is moist. 🖎

Metric Conversion Chart

LIQUID/DRY MEASUREMENTS

¼ teaspoon	1.25 ml
½ teaspoon	2.5 ml
1 teaspoon	5 ml
1 tablespoon	15 ml
1 fluid ounce (2 tablespoons)	30 ml
¼ cup	60 ml
⅓ cup	80 ml
½ cup	120 ml
1 cup	240 ml
1 pint (2 cups)	480 ml
1 quart (4 cups, 32 ounces)	960 ml
1 gallon (4 quarts)	3.84 liters
1 ounce (by weight)	28 grams
1 pound (by weight)	448 grams
2.2 pounds (by weight)	1 kilogram

OVEN TEMPERATURE

Fahrenheit	Celsius	Gas
275	140	1
300	150	2
325	160	3
350	180	4
375	190	5
400	200	6
425	220	7

ABOUT THE AUTHOR

Throughout her life, Shelley Alexander has always had a great love for eating delicious, locally grown, seasonal foods. Shelley grew up in Ohio eating ripe, juicy, vegetables and fruits fresh from her grandparent's extensive garden and the local farmers' markets. This love for eating whole foods and cooking with her mother was the driving force behind her interest and growth in the field of culinary arts. Part of this growth includes formal chef's training at The Los Angeles Culinary Institute.

Shelley is certified as a healing foods specialist. This certification is based on knowing how to utilize traditional, nutrient-dense, organic whole foods to nourish and help restore the body's own natural healing abilities. This holistic and culinary foundation is complemented by a Bachelor of Science Degree in Business Management and Finance from the world renowned Case Western Reserve University in Cleveland, Ohio. Shelley is also certified as a Food Safety Manager by The National Registry of Food Safety Professionals®.

Shelley has many years of work experience in the food and nutrition industry. Shelley has worked in both the restaurant and catering industry as an Executive Chef. Shelley also ran her own successful catering and event planning company Escapade Events. This company provided global cuisine and event services to a wide variety of clients, including top charities and corporations.

Shelley created A Harmony Healing so that she could use her experience, knowledge, and passion to help empower people to make optimal nutrition and lifestyle choices to achieve vibrant health. Her Holistic company A Harmony Healing in Los Angeles, California, provides healing whole foods and anti-aging consultations, Alcat testing, workshops, company health seminars, cooking classes, radiance wellness parties, and holistic supper club events. Her holistic blog has healthy healing foods recipes and easy holistic lifestyle tips.

Shelley's company hosts food demonstrations at top natural food stores in Southern California, including Erewhon Natural Foods Market and Whole Foods Market. Shelley also develops recipes for top whole foods companies whose products she loves and believes in. Go to her Web site and Facebook page for additional recipes, free product giveaways, fun contests, and holistic health tips at: **www.aharmonyhealing.com** and **www.facebook.com/getaharmonyhealing.**

A

Acai Berry Cranberry Tea Sherbet (V) — 223
Acai Berry Cranberry Smoothie (RV) — 89
Aged Balsamic Vinaigrette (RV) — 143
Arugula Comice Pear Salad (RV) — 152
Arugula Spinach Walnut Pesto (RV) — 62

B

Balsamic Brown Butter Grits — 120
Banana Coconut Chia Pudding (V) — 221
Banana Hemp Milk (RV) — 77
Barbecue Sweet Potato Fries (V) — 200
Basic Grits (V) — 120
Basil Alfredo with Zucchini Noodles (RV) — 188
Basil Garlic Spinach — 193
Beef Ragu — 182
Beef Stock — 128
Berries and Cream (RV) — 105
Bing Cherry Smoothie (RV) — 81
Black Rice Pilaf — 190
Blood Orange Coconut Butter (RV) — 61
Blood Orange Maple Dressing (V) — 142
Blood Orange, Ambrosia Apple, and Baby Spinach Salad (RV) — 149
Blueberry Pomegranate Smoothie (RV) — 91
Brown Rice Pilaf — 190
Buckwheat Fruit Granola (V) — 115
Buttermilk Millet Waffles — 117
Butternut Squash Mixed Baby Greens Salad — 158

C

Caramelized Balsamic Onion Scramble — 124
Carob Almond Milk (RV) — 78
Carob Almond Chia Pudding (RV) — 225
Carob Pecan Spread (RV) — 209
Carrot Orange Tonic (RV) — 97
Carrot Pecan Milk (RV) — 72
Carrot Tahini Dressing (RV) — 148
Carrot Walnut Cream Fettuccine (RV) — 186
Chai Pumpkin Oatmeal (V) — 118
Cherry Almond Dressing (RV) — 145
Cherry Goji Berry Smoothie (RV) — 90
Chia Milk Kefir — 96
Chicken Vegetable Quinoa Salad — 151
Chicken Coconut Soup — 140
Chicken Stock — 127
Chive Deviled Eggs — 212
Chocolate Raspberry Smoothie (RV) — 87
Cinnamon Almond Coconut Kefir (RV) — 95
Clarified Butter — 57
Clementine Cassis Dressing (RV) — 144
Clementine Champagne Dressing (RV) — 144
Coconut Milk 2 Ways (RV) — 79
Corn Stock (V) — 130
Cranberry Tuna Salad — 150
Cranberry Quinoa Cereal (V) — 111
Cultured Apple Goji Berry Compote (RV) — 66
Cultured Probiotic Vegetables (RV) — 58
Cultured Tomato Pineapple Salsa (RV) — 65
Cultured Vegetable Dip (RV) — 209

D

Dijon Honey Chicken Wings — 178

E

Encrusted Goat Cheese — 208
E3 Live Melon Elixir (RV) — 94

F

French Toast with Spiced Blueberry Syrup — 113
Fresh and Cultured Mayonnaise — 63
Fudge Goji Berry Truffles (RV) — 217
Fuji Apple Salad — 163

G

Garlic Collard Greens — 194
Goji Berry Kombucha Dressing (RV) — 147

RECIPE INDEX

Grapefruit Kombucha Tea Soda (RV) 98
Green Leaf Lettuce, Tomato, and 121
Onion Scramble

H
Hazelnut Herbal Coffee (V) 97
Heirloom Tomato Cream Dressing (RV) 147
Hemp Seed Herb Salad (RV) 160
3-Herb Pesto (RV) 62
3-Herb Pesto Wild Halibut 176
Honey Dijon Mayonnaise 63
Hot Fudge Sauce (RV) 216

I
Italian Vegetable Salad with Black 159
Pepper Croutons (V)

L
Lamb Chops with Spicy Mint Chutney 183
Lemon Dill Goat Cheese 64
Lemon Ginger Tulsi Tea (V) 99
Lemon Herb Wild Black Cod 173
Lemongrass Ginger Wild Salmon 175
Lime Miso Cornish Game Hens 177

M
Mango Cashew Milk (RV) 75
Mango Chia Ginger Granola (RV) 101
Mango Ginger Dressing (RV) 146
Mango Ice Cream (RV) 220
Mango Raspberry Spirulina 88
Smoothie (RV)
Meyer Lemon Champagne 145
Vinaigrette (RV)
Meyer Lemon Coconut Butter (RV) 61
Meyer Lemon Miso Dressing (RV) 142
Mixed Vegetable Pea Shoots Sandwich (V) 168
Mole Chili 180

Mustard and Turnip Greens with Roasted 198
Baby Turnips

N
Nectarine Smoothie (RV) 91
Nectarine Walnut Milk (RV) 75
Nectarine Yogurt Parfait 109

O
Orange Coconut Yogurt (RV) 103
Orange Ginger Pumpkin Seed Milk (RV) 74
Oven-Dried Tomatoes (V) 60

P
Papaya Ice Cream (RV) 220
Papaya Smoothie (RV) 85
Peach Cucumber Smoothie (RV) 84
Peach Lemonade Elixir (RV) 93
Pear Pomegranate Nut Bowl (RV) 107
Piña Colada Ice Cream (RV) 219
Piña Colada Ice Cream Float (RV) 219
Pineapple Coconut Kefir (RV) 96
Plum Crumble (RV) 226
Pomegranate Millet Pilaf 199
Portobello Mushroom and Grilled Onion 170
Burger (V)

P
Potato Parsley Mash 191
Pumpkin Hazelnut Chai Soup (RV) 133
Pumpkin Raisin Hemp Bread Pudding 227
Pumpkin Seed Spread (RV) 210
Purple Cauliflower Mash 196

R
Rainbow Chard Omelet 123
Raspberry Chocolate Mousse Pie (RV) 215
Raw Beet Tartare (RV) 155

Raw Chocolate Mousse (RV) 214
Raw Corn Chowder (RV) 137
Raw Seed or Nut Cream (RV) 105
Raw Watermelon Jicama Soup (RV) 139
Recipe and Guidelines for Soaking 71
Nuts and Seeds
Red Cabbage Apple Salad (RV) 157
Roasted Chicken Stock 127
Roasted Garlic Coconut Butter (V) 61
Roasted Lemon Fennel and Onions (V) 201
Romaine Tacos (RV) 169

S
Sardine Lettuce Wraps 167
Shitake Mushroom Sauté 192
Slow Braised Beef Roast 185
Slow-Cooked Black-Eyed Peas 197
Smoky Orange Hummus (V) 207
Spiced Maple Syrup (V) 57
Spiced Milk Tea Tonic (V) 99
Spicy Guacamole (RV) 205
Strawberry Banana Maca Smoothie (RV) 84
Strawberry Frozen Yogurt with 218
Balsamic Syrup
Sweet Potato Maple Soup (V) 135
Sweet Potatoes with Coconut 203
Cinnamon Sprinkle (V)

T
Thai Basil Lime Mayonnaise 63
Tomato Basil Cream Soup 131
Tomato Tarragon Goat Cheese 64

V
Vanilla Brazil Nut Milk (RV) 74
Vanilla Cardamom Coconut Kefir (RV) 95
Vanilla Pistachio Milk (RV) 78
Vegetable Marinara Sauce (V) 182
Vegetable Stock (V) 129

W
Watermelon Radish, Golden Beet, 153
and Watercress Salad (RV)
White Balsamic Mayonnaise 63
Wild Blueberry Smoothie (RV) 82
Wild Salmon Patties 172
Wild Salmon Vegetable Rolls 166

Y
Yellow Squash and Basil Omelet 125
Yogurt Goat Cheese and Whey 64
Yuzu Cucumber Salad (RV) 164

Z
Zucchini Onion Sauté (V) 195

Made in the USA
Lexington, KY
23 June 2013